# ISSUES IN PROFESSIONAL COUNSELLOR TRAINING

HALESOWEN COLLEGE
LIBRARY

Windy Dryden,
Ian Horton
and Dave Mearns

097428

074505
361.323DRY
CMC
2weeks.

**Cassell**

Wellington House
125 Strand
London WC2R 0BB

215 Park Avenue South
New York
NY 10003

© Windy Dryden, Ian Horton and Dave Mearns 1995

All rights reserved. No part of this publication may be
reproduced or transmitted in any form or by any means, electronic
or mechanical, including photocoping, recording or any information
storage or retrieval system, without permission in writing
from the publishers.

**British Library Cataloguing in Publication Data**
A catalogue record for this book is available from the British Library

ISBN 0-304-32976-2 (hardback)
0-304-32978-9 (paperback)

Typeset by Falcon Oast Graphic Art
Printed and bound in Great Britain by
Biddles Ltd, Guildford and King's Lynn

KU-316-362

# Contents

Foreword                                                      vi

1   Introduction                                                1
2   The nature of professional counsellor training             12
3   The importance of the core theoretical model               25
4   Staffing and resource issues                               41
5   Admission                                                  55
6   Theory                                                     75
7   Skills training                                            85
8   Self-development                                           97
9   Client work                                               107
10  Supervision                                                117
11  Professional development                                   126
12  Assessment                                                 132
13  Evaluation                                                 145

References                                                     158

Name index                                                     163
Subject index                                                  164

# Foreword

I first trained as a counsellor in 1975. Since that time interest in counselling in Britain has mushroomed. For example, membership of the British Association for Counselling (BAC) continues to grow and training courses in counselling are cropping up everywhere. Fortunately, this growth in the development of counselling in Britain has been paralleled by an increasing concern that counsellors need to be properly trained and their work professionally supervised. The Counsellor Trainer and Supervisor series is designed to reflect this developing interest in the training and supervision of counsellors. It is the first series in Britain devoted to these two important and related professional activities and seeks to provide a forum for leading counsellor trainers and supervisors to share their experience with their novice and experienced colleagues.

In the current volume, Ian Horton, Dave Mearns and myself explore a myriad of issues that need to be considered when establishing a professional counsellor training course. Ian, Dave and myself have, for many years, been involved in the work of BAC's Courses Recognition Group. This group has been concerned with the development of criteria which counsellor training courses have to meet if they wish to be recognized by BAC.

The work that we have done for the CRG has informed the ideas expressed within, but the book should not be seen as representing official BAC policy. We are all experienced trainers in our own right and our views sometimes diverge from current CRG policy. We also point out where the present criteria need to be extended to keep pace with the dynamic growth of counselling and counsellor training.

Windy Dryden

# ONE

# Introduction

This book is for people who are involved or interested in counsellor education and training. We hope it will be a useful reference for trainers, course organizers and prospective students. The book will examine the major issues that need to be addressed when designing and running a professional counsellor training course. It will illustrate and extend the work that the three authors have done on this subject for the British Association for Counselling (BAC) Scheme for the Recognition of Counsellor Training Courses.

In this opening chapter, we will first comment briefly on what we see happening in counsellor training. We will then present our objectives in writing this book and finally we will describe the origin, development and current operation of the BAC courses recognition scheme.

## SETTING THE SCENE

Over the last decade there has been an enormous expansion in counsellor training. According to information in the BAC Directory of Training, between 1987 and 1990 the number of courses in Britain rose from 30 to 90 (Noyes, 1991). Since that time most organizations have increased student numbers and expanded the range of their training, while many other organizations, groups and indeed private individuals have set up new training programmes. A speculative explanation, one that is nonetheless plausible and politically in vogue, could be given in terms of market forces – that is, the expanding provision of training is a response to the escalating demand. At the present time, the well-established courses, especially those officially recognized by BAC, receive many more applications than they have places. For many universities, colleges and other organizations counsellor training has become a growth area. A concomitant explanation is the apparent increase in the demand for counselling. Agencies, especially those offering free or low-cost services, have long waiting lists. Social problems, political trends, and the economic deterioration of the late 1980s and early 1990s, may be reflected in the emergence of counselling within local authority mental health care plans. There has been a similar growth of counselling in primary health care, with an increasing number of GPs recommending counselling to their patients. Alongside that there seems to be greater public awareness of psychological problems. Counselling is frequently mentioned in the popular TV soaps and this may both reflect and contribute to the growing acceptance of counselling as a useful and cost-effective way of dealing with these problems. People with emotional difficulties who previously would have dismissed the idea of counselling may now feel encouraged to seek it.

There is another current trend, which is invariably and quite properly linked with training, and that is the aspirations of many, although certainly not all people who offer their services as counsellors, for professional status and the associated career opportunities with prospects of improved financial security. Professional associations have become involved in seeking to define and regulate professional status. BAC has well-established schemes for the formal recognition of training courses, supervisors and the accreditation of individual counsellors. More recently the United Kingdom Council for Psychotherapy (UKCP) and the British Psychological Society (BPS) have been exploring and setting up procedures for establishing and maintaining appropriate standards of training for psychotherapists and counselling psychologists.

There is a big demand for professional training and a plethora of training opportunities. The increased demand for competent and well-qualified practitioners places a heavy burden of responsibility on those involved in the initial training of professional counsellors.

## OUR OBJECTIVES AND RATIONALE

What is a professional training? This book attempts to answer this question. It seeks to provide a template for the design of counsellor training and elaborates on *The Recognition of Counsellor Training Courses* (1990). This BAC booklet, already in its second edition, has sold widely. Its impact has not only been on established courses wishing to apply for BAC recognition, but also on those thinking about or in the process of setting up counsellor training programmes. It provides the criteria and guidelines for what BAC regards as the minimum standards required for the recognition of in-depth professional counsellor training.

Since the booklet was published, BAC has received many requests for more detailed information, clarification and interpretation of the criteria and guidelines. The aim of this book is to respond to that need by identifying and exploring the critical issues in professional training. Perhaps the key issue is what constitutes the essential and basic elements of a professional training programme. Throughout the book we do our best to maintain what sometimes feels like a precarious balance between, on the one hand, wanting to acknowledge and celebrate the evident richness and diversity of content and approaches to training, while on the other hand, deliberately taking a stand on what we regard as the essential basic elements of a training course. In that respect we remain unashamedly prescriptive. Our central thesis is that effective professional training must include eight basic elements: admission, self-development, client work, clinical supervision, skills training, theory, professional development, assessment and evaluation. We hope that the book will stimulate discussion of the necessary elements.

Chapter 2 discusses what we mean by professional training and contrasts this with other forms of training in counselling. In the third chapter we present the case for professional training courses being based on clearly articulated *core theoretical models*. We will describe what we mean by a core model and consider the implications and common misunderstandings of what we regard as a central aspect of professional training. Chapter 4 deals with the staffing and resource implications of professional counsellor training, while the remaining nine chapters explore the issues relating to each of the eight basic elements in turn, with separate chapters given to the issues of assessment and evaluation.

We hope that the book will encourage trainers to think through issues when planning and setting up training programmes. It may provide a valuable reference point and source of support for those trainers working within larger institutional contexts, trying to negotiate additional resources and time to provide adequate professional training. All too often courses are planned in piecemeal fashion, on shoe-string budgets and with covert institutional pressures to secure a financial return. Professional counsellor training is staff labour-intensive and requires a heavy investment of time and resources. It is not a cheap option for educational expansion. Counsellors are not trained by sitting in large lecture-theatre classes.

Furthermore, although much of counsellor training has hitherto been the province of the smaller private sector organizations that have made such a significant contribution to current values and approaches to training, many courses are now being developed in universities and educational institutions with strong academic traditions. These institutions are often unfamiliar with the ethos and practice of counselling. Current educational trends toward assessment of prior learning, modularization, distance learning, joint teaching across courses, larger staff–student ratios and reduced staff–student contact time represent further challenges within academic settings. While we acknowledge the inevitability and recognize the potential value of some of these innovations, we strike a note of caution in our relatively brief discussions of the possible ramifications for counsellor training. We recognize some very real tensions between quality assurance and economic viability.

## BAC COURSES RECOGNITION SCHEME

### Origin and development 1983–88

The scheme has been successfully operating for seven years following an initial five-year formation period. It was a logical development of the scheme for the accreditation of individual counsellors. The idea was born out of concern about how to help potential students, employers and clients identify high standards of training. In a rapidly expanding marketplace it is difficult for people wanting to apply for counsellor training to decide which courses are likely to provide a good training and lead to professional recognition. Organizations keen to employ counsellors are often ill-informed about the level and quality of training which they should be seeking in applicants for newly created posts.

The initial gestation period was long and hard. The scheme was the product of an elaborate consultation process over several years. The idea was on the agenda of the BAC Accreditation Sub-Committee in the early 1980s. In 1984 a temporary training accreditation committee was formed to explore the possibility of developing some form of accreditation for courses. This planning committee set up a Working Party composed of representatives from a wide variety of counselling orientations, statutory educational institutions, private training and counselling organizations and agencies, together with leading figures from the field of pastoral care and counselling. The task of the Working Party was 'to establish the criteria and the procedure by which BAC could accredit initial courses of training in counselling' (BAC Accreditation Sub-Committee Minutes, 1984).

One of the first dilemmas faced by the Working Party was whether it should be seeking to accredit all forms of initial training, including counselling skills courses. The eventual decision was to focus on those courses whose successful participants might reasonably expect on completion to function as counsellors in formal or, in some cases, informal settings. Such courses were likely, therefore, to be one year full-time or two/three years part-time and to involve in-depth experience and study (BAC, 1990).

Another issue soon emerged within the Working Party. The terms

validation, accreditation and recognition had been used interchangeably. However, unlike the scheme for the accreditation of individual
counsellors the scheme for courses needed to emphasize that the
content, method and approaches may be different, but equally valid,
ways of achieving the same goal. It was important to preserve and
enhance the independence of approaches while at the same time
ensuring that adequate attention was paid to what had been identified
as the core elements of training, irrespective of the varied rationales
underpinning the different courses. The term *recognition* was finally
adopted as the most suitable as it was thought to be less prescriptive
and to reflect greater flexibility in approaches to training.

The initial point of departure for the Working Party was the existing
booklet *Guidance for the ASC Recognition of Training Courses*, produced
by the Association of Student Counselling – a division of BAC. The
Working Party launched an extensive consultation and development process. It soon became apparent that it would be important to seek the
views and participation of the many potentially interested groups –
including validating bodies such as the Council of National Academic
Awards (CNAA), Marriage Guidance Council (MGC), Department of
Education and Science (DES), as well as universities, colleges and private organizations. However, the main thrust of the investigation was to
work alongside existing courses and undertake an in-depth exploration
of approaches to training in a limited, but representative sample of both
new and well-established courses in a variety of educational institutions
and private organizations. Several large training organizations were
approached and other courses offered to participate in response to
advertisements in BAC's *Journal* and *Newsletter*. Five courses par-
ticipated in a three-stage process. The first stage consisted of the
presentation of course brochures, handbooks and training materials.
The second stage involved lengthy discussions with the course tutors,
and in the third stage a team from the Working Party visited each course
to see the training in action, observe sessions and talk to trainees and
other staff. The whole process followed an implicit action research
model. This involved both researchers and subjects in a collaborative
enquiry that worked through several cycles of reconnaissance: fact-
finding, analysis, developing criteria and evaluation. This was followed
by further rounds of reconnaissance and revision through an on-going
spiral of activities, before finally producing the draft plan for the scheme.

The collaborative work with courses was primarily intended to
establish guidelines and criteria for training. Subsequent analysis and
evaluation of the consultation process itself produced guidelines on the
operation and procedure for implementing the actual scheme.

A final draft working paper was produced in 1987. Considering the
diversity of theoretical orientations and disparate experience of Working
Party members, the achievement of consensus was nothing short of

remarkable. Their report and recommendations were presented at an open meeting and favourably received by the 68 people who attended from all over the United Kingdom. It was formally adopted at the BAC annual general meeting in 1987. The Working Party was disbanded, although several members continued to work on the newly constituted Courses Recognition Group (CRG). The CRG was set up as a sub-group of the BAC Accreditation Sub-Committee and was responsible to that sub-committee for the management and operation of the scheme. In October 1988 the CRG membership was appointed. Some people were invited to apply, while others responded to advertisements. In January 1989 the CRG started work on the task of implementing the guidelines and criteria. Three applications had already been received and there was a steady flow of enquiries. By December 1989 the first course was officially recognized by BAC.

## Developments and changes

Like all BAC schemes, the courses recognition scheme is essentially a peer evaluation process. One of the real strengths of the scheme is the built-in self-monitoring and review structures. A representative of every recognized course contributes to the on-going work of the CRG. In this way people who have gone through the process then become a part of it. They give direct feedback on their experience and can thus initiate developments and changes to the scheme.

The scheme identifies the basic elements of counsellor training and sets out to define the minimum criteria for each element. It was essential to set minimum standards for entry into the scheme in order to maintain credibility among counsellors, agencies, trainers, training bodies, students and potential students, clients and would-be clients, other helping professions, government departments and the general public. As previously emphasized, the scheme did not, however, wish to evaluate models or approaches to counselling. It was felt important that the minimum criteria were not constructed in a way that might exclude particular models – including eclectic and integrative approaches. Similarly, the scheme wanted to encourage rather than inhibit fruitful innovation in methods of training. This principle is as strong today, but it did give rise to varying levels of tension and confusion. The whole ethos of the scheme was one of an explorative and educational venture which encouraged genuine dialogue among peers and a great deal of learning on both sides. The ethos of an educational venture among peers remains the essence of the Partnership Stage of the scheme, which will be described later. Nevertheless, the hard reality was that a CRG Panel was a panel of assessors. They had to make a clear decision whether a course satisfied the criteria or not. A course that, for example, did not include supervision or an explicit 'core theoretical model' could not be recognized. Only in this way would the scheme maintain credibility and standards.

The original Working Party, corroborated by feedback from the open meeting, wanted to avoid *quantitative* criteria such as the specification of a required number of hours of theory, client work and supervision or the minimum number of words for written work assignments and so on. This was seen as too rigid and prescriptive. Yet a flood of enquiries from people who had read the first edition of the booklet, as well as from courses trying to assess their eligibility for the scheme, persistently asked for more explicit definition and interpretation of the criteria. What constituted a course of one-year full-time duration or its part-time equivalent? (Some full-time course groups met their tutor only once or twice a week.) What did 'substantial and regular client work' mean? How much written work was regarded as 'adequate'? The early CRG panels experienced great difficulty in evaluating applications against criteria which seemed to need more concrete or explicit interpretation. What has slowly evolved as a product of on-going monitoring and feedback from consumers and CRG members is an attempt to provide operational criteria against which judgements can be made. One example is the 400 hours contact time to define the minimum length of the course. These operational guidelines and interpretations are published as an appendix in the second edition of the BAC booklet.

As the scheme gained maturity other issues emerged. For example, several incidents demonstrated the need for courses to develop a complaints and appeals procedure, and educational trends on modularization and assessment of prior learning have provoked initiatives within the scheme itself. Nevertheless, there is a coherent sense of direction and collective wisdom that achieves a reasonable working balance between 'educational development' and course evaluation – between genuinely celebrating differences and innovation, while at the same time maintaining standards of training.

## HOW THE COURSES RECOGNITION SCHEME WORKS

In the first stage of the process individual courses are encouraged to seek a private consultation with one of the CRG consultants. The scheme does not claim to be suitable for all courses and acknowledges the validity and value of other approaches outside its terms of reference. This initial consultation is intended to clarify eligibility for the scheme and explore what is involved. Consultations vary from short meetings to half-day events. The outcome is not fed back to the CRG and the consultant, taking no part in any subsequent application, remains a consultant to the course rather than a representative of the CRG.

In the second stage, courses wishing to proceed with an application for entry to the scheme produce a detailed submission document. Unlike typical university validation, the scheme is interested not only in the intended aim, rationale, content, structure, methods of learning and teaching, assessment and resources, but equally in the institution's experience of actually delivering the course and the way in which it has used feedback and evaluative data to self-monitor and improve. For this reason, courses need to have worked through and completed at least one cohort of students before applying.

On receiving an application, one member of the CRG management team is appointed to manage the application and check eligibility before appointing a panel of three CRG members: a co-ordinator, who is responsible for organizing the work of the panel, a second member and associate reader – to work with the course. Each panel member will examine a copy of the submission and assess the extent to which it satisfies the criteria for the eight elements. The co-ordinator may request further information or clarification from the course before the panel members make their decision on this 'Application Stage' of the process.

Courses which satisfactorily complete the first step will then be visited by two members of the panel (the co-ordinator and second member) who see the course in action for not less than half a day and usually a full day. This is an opportunity to sit in on skills training sessions, observe supervision groups, meet and discuss the course content and operation with staff and students, examine samples of the students' written work and see the facilities. The visit is seldom awaited without some anxiety and trepidation about getting things right – on both sides – but is typically experienced as stimulating and enormously worthwhile.

As soon as practicable after the visit the panel co-ordinator will prepare a written report on the course's eligibility for recognition. The panel can recommend that the course be recognized, not recognized, or not recognized until specified conditions have been met. This report and recommendation is ratified by the application manager and chair of the CRG.

Successful applications for entry to the scheme achieve BAC-recognized status for the course and are required to participate actively in an on-going consultative partnership with another recognized course over a five-year period. This consultative partnership ensures that courses are both self-monitoring and externally monitored. It is an opportunity to visit, share ideas and discuss their experience of the recognition process and how they responded to suggestions or recommendations made in the original report. The intention is to enhance training standards with consequent benefits to students and thereby, albeit indirectly, to their clients. Every five years courses have to apply for re-recognition. This application includes a report from the consultative partner course – the report plays a critical role in the re-application process.

The scheme is necessarily self-financing. Courses pay incremental fees: an application fee, visit fee and final certification stage fee. Panel members receive a nominal fee and full expenses for their work with each course.

## THE COURSES RECOGNITION GROUP (CRG)

In terms of running the scheme, the CRG is a largely autonomous body. Its membership grows with each newly recognized course. The CRG has a smaller management team appointed from within its membership and meets three times each year to monitor the operation and development of the scheme. The CRG chairperson sits on the BAC Accreditation and Recognition Sub-Committee and reports on the working of the scheme. This helps to ensure compatibility and consistency of standards among the various BAC schemes. It also ensures that, through the sub-committee, the scheme is accountable to the Association and its membership. While the CRG is responsible for the interpretation of criteria and implementation of the scheme, as with any other BAC scheme, the criteria can only be changed by the AGM of the Association.

## RELATIONSHIP BETWEEN ACCREDITATION AND RECOGNITION

The scheme for the *accreditation* of individual counsellors and the scheme for the *recognition* of counsellor training courses are often confused. By satisfactorily completing a BAC-recognized course students or trainees are regarded as having satisfied the education and training requirements for individual counsellor accreditation. This does not mean that they automatically become accredited counsellors. They still have to complete the 450 hours of supervised client work over a period of not less than three years, although this can run concurrently with training. There are obvious advantages in applying for accreditation after having done a recognized course. Completing the application forms is a shorter and simpler process: the detailed analysis of content and hours of training is not required and only one case study, rather than two, needs to be submitted. Furthermore, tutors on recognized courses should be familiar with the accreditation criteria and be able to advise and guide students.

## CONSUMER PROTECTION

A BAC-recognized course is a more readily marketable product and this has obviously motivated many applications, especially in times when competitive market forces are being keenly felt. More important, however, is the explicit consumer protection function of the scheme. Recognized courses need to be organizational members of BAC and course staff required to work within the appropriate BAC Codes of Ethics and Practice for Counsellors, Supervisors and Trainers. In this way a course is directly accountable to BAC and subject to its now well-established complaints and appeals procedure. Any member of the public outside the course, students or would-be students with knowledge of unprofessional or unethical practice or who have any concern about the course, can make a formal complaint which will be thoroughly invest-igated. In addition, recognized courses are now required to have their own student appeals and complaints procedures. Several courses have a standing arrangement with their consultative partner course to provide a mediator or ombudsman to officiate in such situations. In this way a recognized course provides potential consumers with the assurance that any reasonable and justifiable complaints will be listened to and dealt with.

A recognized course also provides consumers with some measure of quality assurance and training standards. Anyone who accepts an offer of a place on a recognized course will know that the course has gone through a rigorous process to gain recognition and, *ipso facto*, that it will include all the basic elements of counsellor training and be participating in an on-going self- and external monitoring process.

## CONCLUSION

What we shall try to do in this book is to explain and develop the guidelines outlined in the BAC booklet *The Recognition of Counsellor Training Courses* (1990). We think that by and large the book will be consistent with the current policy and implementation of the BAC scheme, with which we are all nearing the end of a lengthy involvement at the time of writing. However, it is inevitable that the more detailed discussion of the issues will reflect at least something of our own subjective views and collective 35 years' experience as counsellor trainers. We see it as a strength of the scheme that it is able to accommodate a diversity of views – including our own. We are also aware that the scheme is under continual review, and that approaches to counsellor training are subject to pressure from consumers, organizations, training institutions and professional bodies. Clearly, in writing this book we hope to influence some of these changes and developments.

It is also important to note that this book portrays the *developing* process of courses recognition at a moment in time. Our colleagues in the Courses Recognition Group will help the process to adapt and evolve in the future. Finally, we would like to close this introduction to the book by acknowledging our debt to our CRG colleagues whose work over many years is depicted in this book.

## TWO

# The nature of professional counsellor training

In this chapter we will outline the main elements of professional counsellor training as these have emerged from the work of the Courses Recognition Group (CRG) of the British Association for Counselling (BAC). We will contrast this professional training with other forms of training in counselling and briefly discuss some important issues that arise from recent educational developments and what these might mean for professional counsellor training.

## THE MAIN FEATURES OF PROFESSIONAL COUNSELLOR TRAINING

As we showed in the opening chapter, the BAC Courses Recognition Group was charged with the responsibility of developing a recognition scheme for courses wishing to portray themselves to the outside world as having reached a professional standard of quality that is acceptable to BAC. The level of these courses had to be equivalent to the level of training undertaken by counsellors seeking BAC individual counsellor accreditation. Since the CRG was not asked to look at the quality of short courses, it had to restrict itself to considering courses that were inclusive, i.e. that offered accreditable level and quality training *in toto*. In short, professional counsellor training provides an education and training in counselling to a high level of competence, enabling counsellors to practise safely and effectively with a wide range of clients. Such professionals do require on-going more advanced training, perhaps specializing in work with particular problems and client groups, but they are professionals nonetheless, capable of independent professional practice.

Another crucial point is that professional training as a counsellor involves an in-depth study of a counselling approach based on a core theoretical model. This model, as we shall see in Chapter 3, provides students with an overarching framework within which it is possible to understand a broad range of topics and counselling phenomena.

In wrestling with the question concerning what constitutes professional-level counsellor training the CRG settled on eight basic elements. Since we will elaborate on these elements throughout this book, we will only introduce them briefly here. In doing so we will draw liberally from *The Recognition of Counsellor Training Courses* (BAC, 1990).

## The eight basic elements

1. A professional counsellor training course has a detailed *admissions* policy and selection procedure.

A professional counsellor training course ensures that 'prospective applicants should be provided with detailed information about the course including its structure, aims, contents, assessment requirements, fees and conditions of participation. Applicants should make detailed written applications and provide references from those who know them and their work well. Members of the core course staff should be involved in the selection process which should include some form of interview' (BAC, 1990, p. 4).

During the selection process, staff should consider closely the applicant's potential ability to train as a counsellor in general and in the particular approach to counselling that the course espouses. During this process the selectors 'should seek evidence that an applicant's primary need is not for personal therapy or personal growth' (BAC, 1990, p. 4). The BAC guidelines also state that:

The procedure for selection should be explained clearly and be consistent with the course rationale. Whenever possible, reasons should be given where applicants are rejected after interview. Courses are expected to subscribe to an equal opportunities policy with respect to admission. (BAC, 1990, p. 4)

The issue of admission is discussed more fully in Chapter 5.

2. A professional counsellor training course provides opportunities for on-going *self-development*.

In this respect, the BAC guidelines note that courses should:

(i)    Provide regular and systematic approaches to self-awareness work which is congruent with the course rationale.

(ii)   Ensure that trainees gain experience of being in the client role (beyond that which is created in skills training and role-plays).

(iii)  Ensure that students maintain a 'personal record' which monitors their own self-development. (BAC, 1990, p. 4)

3. A professional counsellor training course stipulates that students should have opportunities for substantial and regular *client work*.

This client work should be understood by the counsellor *and* by the clients as counselling and not some other form of helping, such as providing support or befriending. An absolute minimum of 100 hours of client work is set by CRG and details of this work should be maintained and presented in the form of a written 'professional log'. Client work on professional counsellor training courses is discussed more fully in Chapter 9.

4. A professional counsellor training course ensures that students receive regular *supervision* during the course.

Such supervision should serve three functions:

(a) a training function; (b) a supportive function; and (c) a managerial function (by ensuring that a student's clients are safe). The issue of supervision is discussed in Chapter 10.

5. A professional counsellor training course provides structured opportunities for *skills training*.

As will be discussed in Chapter 7, skills training is a key component of the course curriculum. In the safety of the skills practicum, students can practise with one another the generic skills of counselling as well as the specific skills associated with the core theoretical model that underpins the course. When done well, skills training helps considerably in preparing trainees for client work.

6. A professional counsellor training course provides a thorough grounding in counselling *theory* with special reference to the course's core theoretical model.

Students' learning on theory should include: the explanations, predictions and underlying assumptions of the core theoretical model and a comparison with some other main models in the counselling world. They should also become familiar with the influence of social systems upon behaviour and with viewpoints on the process of change. Finally, students should understand the theoretical basis of any specific client problems that they will encounter as a practitioner.

7. A professional counsellor training course provides opportunities for *professional development*.

Trainees need to understand the major professional codes of ethics and practice and learn how to liaise profitably with helping professionals from other disciplines. In addition, 'courses should provide on-going opportunities for students and staff to meet as a community to reflect on the course as an organization in itself and deal with matters arising' (BAC, 1990, p. 7).

Furthermore, it is deemed to be a responsibilty of staff to remind students that their professional development does not cease when they graduate. To some extent, professional development is an on-going career task.

8. A professional counselling course designs and implements proper *assessment* and *evaluation* procedures.

Assessment differs from evaluation in that the former is concerned with student progress, while the latter attends to the progress of the course. Both assessment and evaluation should be formative and summative (see Chapters 12 and 13) and students should be fully appraised of assessment and evaluation policies at the beginning of the course. Particularly in the case of evaluation procedures, it is likely that students will contribute to their development.

With respect to assessment, the course's core theoretical model will have an influence on what is assessed and how it is to be assessed. Also, in relation to evaluation, the core theoretical model is likely to have a bearing on how the staff meetings and the staff–student community meetings are likely to be conducted. Unlike the authors of the BAC guidelines, we seek to emphasize the difference between assessment and evaluation and regard them as two quite different activities. In this sense, professional counsellor training has nine elements.

Having considered the eight (or nine) main elements of professional counsellor training, let us discuss some of its other features.

## ON PROFESSIONAL COUNSELLOR TRAINING, THE MAIN TRAINING ELEMENTS ARE INTERRELATED

Having outlined the main elements of professional training, we now wish to stress that these are not discrete aspects of training; rather they are linked to one another in important ways. For example, theory should provide a plausible rationale for counselling practice and should be a stimulus for self-development as students explore the personal implications of theoretical material. This is just one example of the interface between some of the different training elements. It is important that trainers provide a suitable model for trainees by emphasizing the interactive nature of the training elements. In addition, it is important that trainees are encouraged to explore for themselves the relationships between the different elements and particularly between such elements as client work, supervision and the core model.

## PROFESSIONAL COUNSELLOR TRAINING IS COHERENT

An important hallmark of professional counsellor training is that it should provide a coherent training experience for students. Since the training elements are interrelated, much attention needs to be paid to how each of these elements contributes to the total training experience. This means that the curriculum requires to be planned and delivered in such a way that the coherence of training becomes apparent to students. If the different elements do not hang together in a coherent manner, then students will not have a broad, balanced training. Rather, they will tend to follow their own interests, ignoring important aspects and missing the opportunity to become rounded professionals.

## PROFESSIONAL COUNSELLOR TRAINING IS BASED ON A CORE THEORETICAL MODEL

The major way that a course can be made coherent is through having a core theoretical model which permeates all aspects of the course. Training in such a model not only helps students to see the links between the different elements, but also provides them with an overall map so that they can see the coherent whole. In addition, a core theoretical model provides an opportunity for students to have in-depth training, otherwise training would be like a smorgasbord, offering bite-size tastes of a large number of different counselling approaches and techniques. At this level of training breadth is not a good substitute for depth.

In the next chapter we will consider the place of the core theoretical model in professional counsellor training in greater detail.

## PROFESSIONAL COUNSELLOR TRAINING IS INTERNALLY CONSISTENT

The core theoretical model also provides a way of ensuring that the elements of a course fit together in an internally consistent manner. This is important since otherwise students would be introduced to contradictory ideas and would end up by being confused, rather than enlightened, by their training.

## PROFESSIONAL COUNSELLOR TRAINING IS INCLUSIVE

One of the reasons why the BAC course recognition scheme was established in the first place was to enable individuals, who would at some later date apply for BAC accreditation, to be secure in the knowledge that their training would be acceptable to BAC. As such, the CRG was only charged with the responsibility of recognizing courses which provided all-inclusive training in the main elements discussed above.

## THE INTEGRITY OF THE TRAINING COHORT IS PRESERVED ON A PROFESSIONAL COUNSELLOR TRAINING COURSE

For students to get the most out of professional counsellor training, they need to experience a consistent, continuous environment in which they can learn to trust one another and, as a result, use and learn from the dynamics of a stable and developing group and involve themselves in the course at a deeply personal level. Only in this way will they get the most out of the training experience. In order for such an environment to be established, students need to stay with one another over the life of the training course and they need to know at the outset that this will be the case. We call this preserving the integrity of the training cohort.

Of course, there will be drop-outs from a course and some students will not proceed to the next year because they have failed the previous year. In exceptional circumstances, individual students may take a year out and re-join the second year of the following cohort. Small changes such as these are not too disruptive of the integrity of a training cohort. What will disrupt such integrity is the situation where students come and go as they construct an individually tailored programme, perhaps comprising different modules from different training institutions. From the perspective of a training course, such fluidity would make it unlikely that sufficient trust would develop among trainees to encourage them to involve themselves personally in the training. The likely result would be that trainees would get a broad training, but one perhaps characterized by blandness and superficiality. This would benefit neither the training course nor individual trainees, who would soon lose any advantage of the greater flexibility derived from 'portable' training and not have the opportunity to benefit from the potentially potent learning that can be gained from participating in a stable and developing group process. Many courses recognize the enormous value of group membership and for this reason insist on a high attendance requirement.

A PROFESSIONAL TRAINING COURSE HAS SENSIBLE STAFF–STUDENT RATIOS

It is possible, at least theoretically, for a course to cover the basic training elements but with an unacceptably high staff–student ratio. The result would be that staff input would be insufficient. Keeping staff–student ratios at sensible levels in the present educational climate of cost-effectiveness and cost-efficiency poses a real challenge to maintaining minimum levels of quality in some aspects of professional counsellor training. This is why courses applying for BAC recognition are asked to demonstrate that their host institution will provide sufficient resources to ensure that quality professional counsellor training will take place.

But what are sensible staff–student ratios on professional counsellor training courses? Let us consider counselling skills training first. Here we suggest a maximum staff–student ratio of one staff member to twelve students. If this ratio was larger then students would receive insufficient staff attention with respect to being observed and being offered feedback on their performance. For group supervision, we recommend a ratio no greater than one supervisor to six students in a weekly group lasting for two and a half hours. This ratio will allow sufficient time for one student to present a case every two weeks. However, if students also receive regular individual supervision, then this ratio could be greater.

When it comes to theory sessions, it might appear at first sight that staff–student ratios are not an issue. However, on professional counsellor training courses with their emphasis on the interactive nature of the basic training, it is important to encourage trainees to explore the practical and personal implications of theoretical material. This necessitates the formation of small groups and while it is unrealistic to expect each small group to have an ever-present staff member to help facilitate the ensuing discussion, it is important that staff members be available to these groups for some of the time. Given this, a staff–student ratio no greater than 1:20 is advocated for theory workshop sessions. Indeed, some such sessions will require additional staffing because they are likely to raise particularly difficult issues for participants. For example, a theory workshop on child abuse would be strengthened by having two or more staff present.

Guidelines on ratios such as we have given should not undermine the BAC course recognition principle that courses are free to establish their own policies, but that they are required to *justify* those policies when seeking recognition.

Finally, the BAC guidelines for the recognition of counsellor training courses stipulate that 'there should be not less than two core members of the training staff for any course' (BAC, 1990, p. 3). By core staff is meant 'those staff who have substantive involvement in admission, assessment, course management and decision-making, as well as teaching/group supervision' (BAC, 1990, p. 22). This means that single-staffed courses are not eligible for recognition. These issues are discussed more fully in Chapter 4 on resources and staffing.

A PROFESSIONAL COUNSELLOR TRAINING COURSE SHOULD HAVE
STAFF–STUDENT CONTACT IN EXCESS OF 400 HOURS

The reader will now appreciate that professional counsellor training courses are very rigorous. Students are expected to make an in-depth study of the core theoretical model, learn a set of generic and approach-specific counselling skills (see Chapter 7), counsel clients, receive on-going supervision of their counselling practice and involve themselves in demanding personal and professional developmental activities. Given this, most counselling courses that have been formally recognized by BAC are much longer than the stated 400-hour staff–student minimum.

The BAC guidelines are clear on which hours can and which cannot be counted towards this stated minimum.

It should be noted that this guidance on course length is in terms of actual staff–student contact hours spent on direct teaching, supervision, individual tutorials and staff/student community meeting time. Coffee or lunch breaks are *not* included. Additional to these hours for each student would be the considerable time required for personal reading, writing, course work assignments, counselling work with clients and personal therapy (if required by the course). These activities are *not* part of the staff–student contact time. (BAC, 1990, p. 21)

## PROFESSIONAL COUNSELLOR TRAINING AND OTHER FORMS OF TRAINING IN COUNSELLING

Another way of clarifying the nature of professional counsellor training is to compare it with other forms of training in counselling. In this section we will briefly consider phased counselling training, counselling skills training and in-house and specialized training in counselling, contrasting these with professional counsellor training.

## The phased approach to training in counselling

There is an approach to counselling training which is based on the idea that such training occurs in phases. In this approach a student would, for example, begin with an introductory course, proceed to a diploma course and end up with a Masters level or advanced course. We have no serious qualms with this approach – which we call 'phased counselling training' – if it proceeds in a logical stepwise fashion and if an individual student receives training equivalent to what is available on a recognized counsellor training course.

As we mentioned above, an advantage of phased counselling training from the student's perspective is that their qualifications are portable. Thus, they may complete an introductory course at institution X, continue with a diploma course at training organization Y and receive a Masters from university Z. The major obstacle to phased training is the absence of nationally agreed standards of training in counselling at each level. For example, a course which may be awarded a diploma at one institution may only merit the award of a certificate at another. In addition, even if two diploma courses, for example, are equivalent in curriculum coverage, it does not follow that they are equivalent in quality. Thus, one diploma course may be well taught by highly qualified staff, whereas the other diploma may be poorly taught by staff who are barely more experienced than their students. If there were nationally agreed training standards at each level and a recognition procedure for courses also at each level, then we would have more faith in the quality of training a student might receive following a phased route, particularly if it could be shown that students had studied a core theoretical model in depth over the entire phased period. However, the present haphazard state of affairs of counselling training in Britain (which, in part, prompted BAC to initiate its course recognition procedure) means that one student may receive excellent training from a phased programme of courses while another might receive training of lamentable quality. At present, we have no formal machinery to discriminate between the two.

An additional problem concerns a number of Masters courses in counselling. Such courses may require some prior training from students, but may not then provide sufficient training themselves to match the in-depth quality of training on offer from BAC-recognized courses. The danger is that such Masters courses, with their heavy emphasis on academic study and research, become courses *about* counselling rather than courses which provide training *in* counselling.

The worrying point for us is that students graduating from a recognized counsellor training course – which at present is most likely to award a diploma – will be better trained than someone who has completed such a Masters degree, but students will appear to the outside world as *less* highly qualified! This may seem to represent a chaotic picture, but it simply mirrors competing demands for time within higher education (Dryden, 1994a).

## Counselling skills training

BAC makes an important distinction between counsellors and those who use counselling skills in the service of their predominant work role (for example, social workers, health workers and teachers). As a discrete activity, the function of counselling skills training is to help equip this latter group with counselling skills which can be used in their work role. As such, the amount of theory on counselling skills courses is kept to a minimum and is designed to help students see the purposes of the skills which they are required to learn. While such courses encourage students to involve themselves in self-development activities, these tend to be restricted to the acquisition of the skills themselves.

By contrast, when counselling skills training is part of a professional counsellor training course, its function is to help train professional counsellors.

## In-house and specialized counselling training courses

In-house and specialized counselling training courses both have as their goal the preparation of people who will either counsel in a specific counselling agency or work with defined client groups.

When a counselling agency runs an in-house counselling course, it does so either because its directors are unhappy about the prior training of potential volunteers or, more likely, because they wish its counsellors to work in a certain way and believe that the agency itself is best placed to provide such training. When such in-house courses contain all the elements of professional counsellor training, these are usually covered in less depth than on professional courses. Such courses can be regarded as embryonic professional training courses; indeed, some recognized courses started life as in-house training courses.

However, most in-house training courses do not seek to cover all the elements of professional counsellor training, paying most attention to counselling skills training and supervised counselling as well as some theory and self-development work.

The rationale of specialized counselling courses is to help prepare people to work with specific client groups (such as the bereaved and people with HIV/AIDS). Since the goal of such courses is narrow, their curricula are necessarily restricted and all the training activities are geared to helping students counsel the targeted client group. As such these courses, however excellent they may be, are usually much shorter and lighter on assessment than professional counsellor training courses since they have very different aims from professional courses.

## POSSIBLE FUTURE DEVELOPMENTS

While we have outlined the basic elements of professional counsellor training as stated in the guidelines of the BAC course recognition scheme, we wish to stress that this is not the last word in professional counsellor training and the nature of such training is likely to change as the profession of counselling changes. Change does not only arise from development *within* the profession. In the final section of this chapter we shall consider, first, a number of developments in *education* which press for changes in the BAC guidelines and, second, the possibility that the guidelines will have to pay more attention to *research* in order to maintain professional credibility. While the first of these is being actively considered by the Courses Recognition Group, the second is for the near future.

### Professional counsellor training and educational developments

A number of recent developments in education have implications for professional counsellor training as defined by the CRG. Indeed, the CRG has set up a working party to consider the Assessment of Prior Learning and its implications. At the time of writing, this working party has provided its initial report recommending procedures, including a pilot study to implement APL. Nevertheless, what we have to say here about the effect of these educational developments remains speculative.

*Credit Accumulation Transfer Scheme (CATS).* This scheme is based on the idea that students can accumulate educational 'credits' (often in the form of points-earning modules), which they can transfer from one institution to another. In this way they can gain a qualification to suit their changing circumstances or desired rate of training without being committed to a single, inclusive period of study.

This scheme threatens two basic principles of professional counsellor training. First, it threatens the inclusive nature of professional training where all the basic elements of such training are provided on a single course. Second, it threatens the principle of the integrity of the training cohort where a single cohort of trainees trains together on a single course. However, CATS does not prohibit a person from applying for individual counsellor accreditation from BAC, since at present the accreditation scheme will accept programmes of training that are non-BAC-recognized as long as there is at least one substantial and coherent period element of training within the programme.

*Accreditation of Prior Learning (APL).* APL involves a student seeking exemption from part of a course. This is done by providing evidence of past study or experience that demonstrates the student is already competent in that part of the course. In doing so the student submits a portfolio comprising such evidence, which might include projects, assignments, letters of validation, written work, videos or tapes.

The use of APL on professional counselling training courses threatens the integrity of the training cohort in a different way from the threat posed by CATS. In CATS, students threaten cohort integrity by going from institution to institution, while in the APL scheme students do so by not taking part in one or more of the various training activities on a single course. As such, the development of a course identity is compromised. However, the CRG is currently grappling with these issues and it seems likely that some form of APL will be recognized in the future.

*National Vocational Qualifications (NVQs) and Scottish Vocational Qualifications (SVQs).* In 1992 the Advice, Guidance and Counselling Lead Body (AGCLB) was set up to develop national standards for people who provide advice, guidance and counselling as a major part of their work role. The standards comprise a description of units or sets of competencies grouped round a major work activity, of elements or statements of what a competent person should be able to do, of performance criteria that define the acceptable level of performance for the element and of range indicators which state the circumstances in which the competence applies (AGCLB, 1994).

At the time of writing, NVQs and SVQs have not been developed to cover professional-level counsellor training and it is not clear what the implications of this government-sponsored initiative will be for professional counsellor training or the BAC courses recognition scheme.

## Research

At present, professional counsellor training courses do not have to require students to carry out a piece of research, nor indeed do they have to provide students with training to help them become informed consumers of the research literature in counselling. However, this may change in the near future. Counselling psychology has recently been awarded divisional status in the British Psychological Society, and Masters- and doctorate-level training programmes in the subject, with their strong emphasis on research, are now on offer. The possible outcome of this development is that counselling psychologists may be more attractive to employers than counsellors because of the former's expertise in research. This pressure may grow as employers become increasingly accountable to undertake audit and other forms of evaluation.

If this possible scenario becomes reality, then we predict that professional training courses in counselling will be asked to provide research modules on their curricula. If this happens, the CRG will have to include research as an additional training element. We use the word 'additional' advisedly since it is very unlikely that the CRG would seek to compromise the quality of professional counselling courses by recommending the removal of any existing training element or by suggesting that courses spend less time on these elements to make way for the inclusion of research components. This means that, in the future, recognizable professional counselling courses may well be longer than at present. However, some counsellor training courses already include training in how to evaluate the outcomes of counselling practice and how to understand and evaluate the counselling research literature, so the development may not present particular problems.

We have been considering possible future changes in the nature of professional counsellor training. Whatever changes are made, however, in our view such courses will still have to be informed by a core theoretical model. In the next chapter we will consider the importance of this central feature of professional counsellor training.

# THREE

# The importance of the core theoretical model

In this chapter we will consider a central feature of professional counsellor training: the core theoretical model. We will discuss its nature and function and show the impact that it has on the basic elements of professional training outlined in the previous chapter. We will also consider the special issue of integrative and eclectic core models.

## THE NATURE OF A CORE THEORETICAL MODEL

### The BAC position

A recognized professional counsellor training course as defined by the BAC Courses Recognition Group (CRG) provides in-depth training for intending professional counsellors. The guidelines for the recognition of counsellor training courses (BAC, 1990) state that such in-depth training 'should provide a coherent grounding for the student in a core theoretical model of counselling' (BAC, 1990, p. 3).

It elaborates on this statement thus:

> The 'core theoretical model' of a course may be Behavioural, Psychodynamic, Gestalt, Person-Centred, etc. It is important that the course really does focus in depth on this theoretical model, taking students towards the limits of theory, practice and research. It is not simply a matter of, for instance, expecting students to take a 'broadly person-centred' approach with clients. If the core theoretical model is 'Person-Centred' then that model has to permeate all the course

elements. (BAC, 1990, p. 22)

## Theories of personality and counselling

Most approaches or models of counselling have in some way been spawned by one of the broad psychological schools of personality and are often regarded as synonymous with them. Reber (1985, p. 533) describes personality as a term resistant to definition and so broad in usage that no simple coherent statement about it can be made. Although the approaches to personality differ widely, the various theories seek to describe those characteristics of a person that account for consistent patterns of behaviour and to explain how the normal variations of personality develop. Another function of theories of personality is to provide an explanation for the development and assessment of psychological disorders or psychological problems. Many theories of personality suggest, with varying degrees of clarity and detail, methods of psychological treatment which imply particular approaches to counselling. Yet, in themselves, do theories of personality provide an adequate theoretical underpinning for counselling practice? The link between personality theories and counselling seems tenuous at best. Fonagy and Higgitt (1984) and others (for example, Mahrer, 1989) challenge the validity of this often assumed link. They suggest that even if a theory of personality contains a very clear explanation as to how a disorder arises it does not follow that a method of treatment based on that theory will be developed or that it is possible to identify the ways in which it would be internally consistent with that specific theory rather than any other.

The growing interest in integrative approaches seems to have given impetus to the discussion about what comprises a theory of counselling. Nelson-Jones (1985, p. 131) states that theoretical models of counselling should contain a statement of basic assumptions, an explanation both of the origin of functional and dysfunctional feelings, thoughts and behaviours and of the ways in which they are perpetuated or sustained, together with internally consistent practical suggestions for change. It is a useful analysis, providing an attractively simple and easy to apply operational framework for a model or a theory of counselling. Nevertheless, it seems to go little further than an analysis of the components of a theory of personality. It is not explicit about what the basic assumptions need to refer to and provides no guidelines on the nature or type of practical suggestions for change or the criteria for internal consistency. Beitman (1992) is critical of the efforts to develop theories of personality and what he sees as the emphasis placed on the need to account for the genesis of psychological problems. He argues that as counselling is essentially a practical endeavour intended to help people change, much greater attention should be given to the factors that maintain psychological difficulty and the process of change connected to practical goals.

Mahrer (1989) unequivocally states that a theory of personality is not the same as a theory of counselling. He argues that the components are different and so too are the issues and questions with which they are concerned. He proposes that any theory of counselling should contain seven components (1989, p. 33):

1. Useful material to elicit from clients.
2. How and what to listen for and observe.
3. Explanatory frameworks for client presenting problems and selected targets for change.
4. Therapeutic goals and directions for change.
5. General and more concrete principles for change.
6. Strategies, techniques and procedures for intervention.
7. Explanation of what strategies to use under what circumstances or conditions.

Mahrer gives a detailed description of each component, but does not differentiate between them adequately. The complexity of his ideas make his model relatively inaccessible.

## 'Model' or 'theory' of counselling

Like most other counselling texts, we have used the terms model and theory loosely, almost interchangeably. There is considerable disagreement among social scientists about the precise relationship between these concepts. A model describes a system of beliefs and can be defined as an 'abstraction of observables' (Beitman, 1990). A model seeks to represent the supposed structure of how counselling is thought to work and provides a series of tentative propositions or basic assumptions as a framework to conceptualize counselling. A theory is primarily an attempt to explain causation and predict what will happen. Reber (1985, p. 769) defines a theory as a complete and coherent characterization of a well-articulated domain of investigation. It provides a set of interrelated principles that is put forward as an explanation of known facts and empirical data. Even with a pragmatic interpretation of this definition, most approaches to counselling are not described in a way that adequately satisfies this definition. We believe that students need to recognize that the importance of theory is to help them to understand what might happen with clients as opposed to what has to happen or what will happen. In this sense we prefer to retain the concept of a *model* rather than a theory of counselling.

## A core theoretical model for BAC course recognition

Hansen *et al.* (1982, p. 17) helps us to understand the criteria for an acceptable core theoretical model for the purposes of course recognition. They say that a good core theoretical model has the following characteristics:

1. *Clarity*. A good core theoretical model 'must be easily understood and communicable. Its assumptions or hypotheses must be stated so as not to contradict one another.'
2. *Comprehensiveness*. A good core theoretical model 'is comprehensive. It does not deal with exceptions or isolated cases, but supplies plausible explanations for a variety of phenomena in a variety of situations.'
3. *Heuristic*. A good core theoretical model 'is heuristic in nature; it is stated in terms explicit enough to generate research. If it is a vague accumulation of thoughts, it is inaccessible to testable hypotheses. It must be so designed that it can be subjected to the rigors of scientific inquiry.'
4. *Means–ends related*. A good core theoretical model 'should relate means to the desired outcomes, stating techniques for achieving the end product'. This means that a core theoretical model needs to have a clear idea of healthy human functioning and specify counselling procedures designed to help clients achieve this level of functioning.
5. *Usefulness*. A good core theoretical model 'is useful to its intended practitioners . . . to the counselor it is one that supplies adequate guidelines for the use of specific techniques for individual clients'.

While the established core theoretical models may adequately satisfy these criteria, suggested models based on eclectic or integrative rationales devised by course tutors have to prove that they meet them before they can be regarded as acceptable core theoretical models for the courses based on them. We will discuss eclectic and integrative core models later in this chapter.

## THE FUNCTION OF THE CORE THEORETICAL MODEL

Essentially the core theoretical model strengthens a course by offering a skeleton structure which permeates the course and offers support and integration among all its elements.

## THE CORE THEORETICAL MODEL PROVIDES AN OVERALL FRAMEWORK IN WHICH TRAINEES CAN UNDERSTAND THE DIFFERENT ELEMENTS OF THE COURSE

Professional counsellor training is very demanding for trainees. They have to study in depth the theoretical ideas underpinning their counselling work, learn a set of generic and specific counselling skills, see clients under supervision and involve themselves in a broad range of self-development and professional development activities. Without some overarching framework within which trainees can make sense of these disparate elements, they would become very confused, a state which would interfere significantly with their learning and practice with clients. It is not sufficient that the core theoretical model is presented to students. Trainees need to be able to articulate the model if they are to get the most out of studying it. Consequently, courses need to develop ways of assessing the extent to which students are successful in articulating the core model (see Chapter 12 on assessment). In only 400/450 hours of training it is not possible for students to achieve a level of safe and effective practice in more than one basic approach. Counsellors-in-training need the security of in-depth training in one basic approach as a prerequisite of study and practice in other approaches.

### THE CORE THEORETICAL MODEL PERMEATES THE COURSE

As defined by the course recognition group, professional counsellor training is a comprehensive experience. If students are to make an in-depth study of one major counselling model it needs to permeate the course. As such, each element needs to be consistent with the core theoretical model. To use an analogy, the core theoretical model is like the hub of a wheel linking together the different elements of the curriculum (or spokes). For example, if the core theoretical model of a course is Rational Emotive Behaviour Therapy, and students are learning about the theoretical importance of irrational beliefs in human dysfunctioning, then they will be encouraged to identify their own irrational beliefs in self-development exercises and they will learn ways of identifying and challenging them as they become manifest both in the skills training component and in client work.

### THE CORE THEORETICAL MODEL PROVIDES A RATIONALE FOR THE INTERACTIVE COURSE ELEMENTS

Most counselling approaches emphasize the holistic nature of human beings and the fact that different aspects of being human are related to one another. In the same way, the different elements of counsellor training are interrelated and this interactive concept should be reflected in the design and running of a professional counselling course. The core theoretical model provides a rationale for the interactive nature of these elements. For example, on a Person-Centred course, trainees may study in the theoretical component of the course the ways in which people distort experiences in line with a negative self-concept. Then, in the same session, students may break into small groups to reflect on ways in which they may distort their own experiences based on their own negative self-concept. Note that this latter work fits best under the heading of self-development, but it takes place in the timetabled theory part of the course. The core theoretical concept provides the content for both types of activities and therefore the link between them.

## THE CORE THEORETICAL MODEL PROVIDES A MODE OF RELATING BETWEEN COUNSELLOR AND CLIENT AND BETWEEN TRAINER AND TRAINEE

A core theoretical model outlines a way in which counsellors should relate to their clients. Different core theoretical models posit different ways of relating to clients (Lambert, 1982). Since most trainers would subscribe to the view that they have an important role to play in facilitating the personal and professional development of their trainees, it follows that the way in which trainers interact with their students should be influenced by the core theoretical model. This should not only be apparent when self-development and professional development are formally on the course agenda, but it should also be manifest in the way staff treat their students at other times (e.g. during admission procedures, in theory sessions, during assessment and evaluation exercises and in informal contacts). Thus, if a course is Person-Centred, one would expect trainees to experience their trainers as empathic, respectful and genuine in their encounters with them, since these three 'core conditions' are set out by the Person-Centred core model as being necessary and sufficient for the growth of clients and therefore trainees.

However, since the core theoretical model should influence staff–student relationships this should also be apparent in the ways in which trainees treat their trainers. Thus, on a successful Person-Centred course staff should also experience their students as empathic, respectful and genuine in the way students interact with them. This should be more apparent in the latter phase of the course than in the early phase, when students have not yet internalized the core theoretical model.

Because the core theoretical model is such an important feature of professional training, it is essential that staff are properly trained in it. This may appear self-evident, but courses which have applied in the past for course recognition have had core staff who were either not properly trained in any model or had been properly trained, but in a different core model! Since this point is not obvious, let us repeat it.

*Because the core theoretical model is such an important feature of professional training, it is essential that staff are properly trained in it.* We will discuss the issue of staff more fully in the next chapter.

## THE INFLUENCE OF THE CORE THEORETICAL MODEL ON THE COURSE ELEMENTS

As we argued above, a core theoretical model should permeate a professional counsellor training course and its influence should be present throughout the course. In this section, we will briefly discuss the way a core theoretical model influences each basic element of professional training.

### The influence of the core theoretical model on theory

The core theoretical model influences much of the content of the theory part of the course. First, trainees have to study the core theoretical model in depth and understand its stance on a variety of issues. The following is an illustrative list of eight such issues.

1. ASSUMPTIONS ABOUT THE NATURE OF BEING HUMAN

Wallace (1986) outlines eleven basic issues that tease out a core theoretical model's assumptions about being human. His framework, or one similar, is useful to help students understand the model's position on this philosophical point. Wallace's eleven issues ask the following questions:

- To what extent is our behaviour determined by conscious factors and to what extent by unconscious factors?
- To what extent do we have freedom of choice over the way we act and to what extent is our behaviour conditioned?
- Are we more influenced by social determinants or by biological determinants?
- What weight does the core theoretical model place on our uniqueness as humans and what weight on our sense of commonality with others?
- To what extent are we shaped by our early experiences and to what extent by our later, on-going experiences?
- Are we more influenced by real events or by our psychological appraisal of these events?
- How does the core theoretical model explain the way we learn?
- How important is the 'self-concept' in the model's explanation of our development?
- To what extent is membership of a group on the one hand,

and solitude on the other, important for mental health?
- Which motivational concepts does the core theoretical model use in its explanation of the determinants of behaviour and what weight does it assign to these concepts?
- How important is the concept of reward in the core theoretical model's explanation of the determinants of behaviour?

## 2. THE NATURE OF PSYCHOLOGICAL DISTURBANCE AND WELL-BEING

Most core theoretical models advance a view on the nature of psychological disturbance and well-being and have a set of concepts to explain the existence of each. It is important that students have an accurate understanding of the core model's view on this issue.

## 3. HOW PSYCHOLOGICAL PROBLEMS ORIGINATE AND ARE MAINTAINED

Some core theoretical models place much store on the importance of understanding how clients' problems originate, while others regard this as unimportant or irrelevant to the counselling process. In accounting for the maintenance of these problems, some models stress intrapsychic factors, while other models place more emphasis on interpersonal factors. It is important that students understand the core theoretical model's position on this important issue.

## 4. HOW PERSONAL CHANGE TAKES PLACE

An understanding of how the core theoretical model conceives of the way people change is crucial if students are to understand why different counselling interventions are suggested at different times. It also helps them to appreciate how quickly or slowly change is expected to take place and what obstacles can be expected along the way.

## 5. THE PROCESS OF COUNSELLING

Linked to the concept of how people change is an understanding of the process of therapeutic change. While there are many views of the process of counselling, we will briefly discuss Beitman's model (1987) since this not only allows students to understand the core theoretical model's view on this issue, it also permits a comparison between the core model's stance on the counselling process and that of other counselling approaches.

Beitman (1987) argues that there are four basic stages in the process of counselling:

- *Engagement.* In the engagement stage, the counsellor and client strive to form a working alliance with one another.
- *Pattern search.* In this stage, the counsellor and client work together to identify patterns of thought, feeling and behaviour which account for the client's problem. At this stage, the core theoretical model's specific concepts come to the fore (e.g. irrational beliefs in Rational Emotive Behaviour Therapy).
- *Pattern change.* Here, the counsellor helps the client to relinquish old patterns and initiate and strengthen new patterns.
- *Termination.* The counsellor helps the client to prepare for the end of counselling and to maintain the changes achieved.

Beitman also makes the point that each stage is composed of six elements:

1. *Goals.* These define the objectives of each stage (as described above).
2. *Techniques.* These are the means by which the objectives of each stage may be met. It is here that different core theoretical models stress approach-specific ways of achieving these goals.
3. *Content.* While there may be general themes that most models acknowledge, it is here that the core theoretical model influences what is discussed (e.g. irrational beliefs in Rational Emotive Behaviour Therapy, ego states in Transactional Analysis, etc.).
4. *Resistance.* This describes the ways in which clients 'resist' the influence of their counsellor and their own therapeutic goals.
5. *Transference.* This describes the tendency of clients to view the counsellor in idiosyncratic ways influenced by their unresolved issues with significant others.
6. *Counter-transference.* This describes the same tendency as above from the perspective of the counsellor.

Using this framework (or one like it), the trainer would help students understand the core theoretical model's stance on the phases and the elements within each phase.

6. COMPARISON BETWEEN THE CORE THEORETICAL MODEL AND OTHER COUNSELLING MODELS

While it is important that students on a professional counsellor training course study in depth one core theoretical model, it is also important that they have some knowledge of other approaches to counselling. Otherwise, students get the false impression that the core theoretical model represents the only valid way of conceptualizing and responding therapeutically to clients' concerns. In addition, the study of other counselling approaches helps students to see the possible limits of the course's core model and to develop their critical powers as they undertake to compare and contrast their core model with theoretical models advocated by other professional counselling courses. While it is not possible for students on professional counselling courses to study more than one model in depth, knowledge of others means that they can talk intelligently with practitioners and students from other approaches and hence gain a sense that they are a part of a wider counselling community. Ignorance of all counselling approaches other than one's own encourages the unhealthy state of isolationism and omnipotence, which we believe is detrimental to the development of counselling as a profession.

## 7. THE THEORETICAL BASIS FOR ANY SPECIFIC CLIENT PROBLEMS OR ISSUES INCLUDED ON THE CURRICULUM

Students on professional counselling courses need to understand how to make sense of the problems and issues that clients discuss in counselling. The core theoretical model provides such understanding. If the core theoretical model cannot account for such problems and issues, its limitations should be noted and alternative explanations studied.

Some core theoretical models (e.g. the existential approach to counselling) do not focus on specific client problems but prefer to consider major themes which culminate in a variety of problems. Since the BAC Course Recognition procedure is flexible and does not seek to place all courses into a Procrustean bed, it can accommodate the theoretical ideas of core theoretical models on such a point.

## 8. THE SOCIAL SYSTEMS IN WHICH WE LIVE

It is deemed important that professional counselling training courses study the social systems in which we live as these affect client development and counselling practice. As the recognition guidelines make clear, 'the term "social systems" is taken to include such factors as race, culture, gender, sexual preference, politics and ethics' (BAC, 1990, p. 6).

Core theoretical models differ concerning the extent to which they seek to explain the workings of social systems. Thus, Psychodynamic theory seeks to account for the functioning of organizations (Menzies, 1970) and the political dimension of the human psyche (Samuels, 1993), amongst others, and Person-Centred theory provides a rationale for the resolution of cultural conflict, for example (Rogers, 1977, 1982). Cognitive-Behavioural theory, on the other hand, has restricted itself to explaining clinical phenomena and its theorists have resisted the attempt to extend its range of convenience beyond the consulting room

(Dryden, 1994b). Whether or not a core theoretical model has made an attempt to explain the functioning of social systems or theorize about social issues, all courses will have to draw upon social science disciplines to understand fully the social context of counselling. Indeed, they are encouraged to do so by the BAC course recognition guidelines. It is generally recognized, then, that no core theoretical model can adequately explain the impact of social factors on client development and counselling practice.

## The influence of the core theoretical model on counselling skills training

The core theoretical model has an influence on both the content of skills training and the way it is approached. Let us consider the content of such training first. As will be discussed further in Chapter 7, most approaches to counselling would agree on the importance of teaching a range of counselling skills (e.g. active listening, empathic responding, etc.). These may be termed generic skills since they are widely accepted, although the purpose of using such skills will vary from model to model. So with respect to generic skills the core theoretical model affects the purposes for which the skills are used more than the skills themselves. Where the core theoretical model does influence the nature of the skills taught in this component of counsellor training is with what might be called approach-specific skills. These skills are closely allied to the core theoretical model and are used to achieve the counsellor's objectives which are again specific to this model (e.g. Socratic disputing of irrational beliefs to help the client to think more rationally in Rational Emotive Behaviour Therapy).

With respect to how skills training is approached, the influence of skills training is best seen when we compare models which place a lot of stress on the use of skills and techniques (e.g. the 'skilled helper' model of Egan (1994) and Cognitive-Behavioural counselling (Trower *et al.*, 1988)) and models which de-emphasize techniques, placing more stress on the therapeutic value of the counsellor's attitude (e.g. Existential counselling (Deurzen-Smith, 1988) and Person-Centred counselling (Mearns and Thorne, 1988)). In short, the first two models take a more technical approach to skills training than the last two.

## The influence of the core theoretical model on client work

It would be surprising indeed if the core theoretical model did not have a strong impact on the student's client work. Thus, if the student was practising Cognitive-Behavioural counselling on a Person-Centred course, one would ask some deeply searching questions about what was going on. So, assuming that students' counselling practice is consistent with the core theoretical model, we need to consider the impact of the core model on the context in which students' practice takes place. Since this issue is fully discussed in Chapter 9, we will just 'flag' it here as a point to be aware of when designing or evaluating a professional counsellor training course.

## The influence of the core theoretical model on supervision

It is essential that there is consistency between client work and supervision. If students' casework is based on the Psychodynamic core model, then their supervisors should operate from a Psychodynamic perspective. There may be practical difficulties in arranging this, however. For example, a course may be located in a part of the country where there may not be sufficient supervisors who work in a way that is consistent with the course's core model. The temptation, in such a case, is to make use of supervisors from a different therapeutic orientation. We believe that this temptation should be firmly resisted, otherwise the course will not be providing an internally consistent training experience which is an important hallmark of professional counsellor training.

The question also arises concerning how *close* the match should be between the core theoretical model and the supervision. Ideally, the match should be exact, but what if it is not? Would an Object Relations supervisor be acceptable on a Freudian course or a Cognitive-Behavioural supervisor on a Rational Emotive Behaviour Therapy course? The BAC Courses Recognition Group does not have precise guidelines for these situations. It would depend on how important the specific core model (e.g. Freudian) was to the course as opposed to the broad core model (e.g. Psychodynamic). The more a course relies on a specific core model within the broader tradition whence it comes, the more important it would be for supervisors to come from the same specific core model as that which permeates the course.

## The influence of the core theoretical model on self-development

The core theoretical model also gives shape to the self-development activities in which students are asked to participate. Several courses require trainees to be in personal therapy during the whole or part of the course. Clearly, it is essential that the type of personal therapy should be consistent with the core theoretical model. This sometimes causes dilemmas for students. For example, a student recently entered on a Gestalt training course was required to enter Gestalt therapy and terminate work with a Rational Emotive Behaviour Therapist. While the course was perfectly correct in its guideline on this point, the student lost out on what for him was a very positive personal experience. This example should remind us that undertaking professional counsellor training involves costs as well as benefits.

Other self-development activities should reflect the influence of the core theoretical model on the student's personal development. Thus, a trainee's personal journal on a Rational Emotive Behaviour Therapy (REBT) course should contain frequent mention of the way the theoretical concepts underpinning REBT are being applied to personal learning. The student should consider the role of irrational beliefs, low frustration tolerance and lack of self-acceptance in his personal experiences and relationships with others. If his journal contains no reference to such issues, but is full of references to concepts from the Psychodynamic core model, something is going wrong in that person's training or in the course itself. So, consistency between the 'spoke' of self-development and the 'hub' of the core theoretical model is again the most important criterion to be met on this issue.

## The influence of the core theoretical model on professional development

As will be discussed fully in Chapter 11, a professional counsellor training course attends to the professional development of its students. One example of the way that the core theoretical model particularly influences professional development is in the way course community meetings are run. On an REBT course, for example, there would be an agenda of items to be discussed and the interaction between staff and students would be fairly informal in nature, while on Person-Centred and Psychodynamic courses such meetings would be far less structured; the main difference being that on a Person-Centred course, the staff would offer more of an I–Thou relationship than on the latter, where staff would be more likely to take an interpretive role in relation to the group dynamics.

## The influence of the core theoretical model on admission

As will be mentioned in Chapter 5, it is essential that potential students know as much about the course as possible. In particular, they need to have a clear idea about the core theoretical model that underpins and permeates it. With respect to issues concerning the core model, admission tutors need to consider two questions. First, have applicants read sufficiently about the core theoretical model to indicate that they have made an informed decision by applying? Second, is the applicant suitable for training in the core theoretical model? To answer this second question admission tutors must have a clear idea of the characteristics of effective counsellors in the counselling approach that the course is based upon. If these criteria are kept clearly in mind at interview then the applicant's potential to become such a practitioner can be assessed using a variety of procedures (see Chapter 12). If the applicant is not suitable for training in the core theoretical model, but the admission tutors consider that he has potential for training in another counselling approach then such a viewpoint should be offered.

Finally, the way the admission procedures are carried out should be consistent with the core theoretical model's viewpoint concerning how people should be treated. (It should be borne in mind, however, that applicants should not be counselled!)

## The influence of the core theoretical model on assessment and evaluation

Finally, as we shall point out in Chapters 12 and 13, the student assessment and course evaluation procedures should be carried out in accordance with the core theoretical model. For example, certain core models (e.g. Behavioural and Cognitive-Behavioural counselling) place much emphasis on objective measures of client progress, while others (e.g. Person-Centred and Existential counselling) place more store on subjective measures, and eclectic approaches would use a variety of measures of the progress clients have made. These differences should be reflected in both measures of student progress and course evaluation.

Currently, educational institutions are having to satisfy wider pressures of quality assurance which tends to favour more objective measures. Thus, some courses will have to compromise on this issue, but should still remain as faithful to their core theoretical model on this point as they can.

## INTEGRATIVE AND ECLECTIC CORE THEORETICAL MODELS

A major development in the fields of counselling and psychotherapy has been the increasing attention given to the issues of integration and eclecticism (see Dryden, 1992, for a full discussion). As a reflection of this trend, more and more courses are applying for course recognition stating that their core theoretical model is eclectic or integrative in nature. BAC course recognition panels investigating such courses found considerable variation in the coherence of the training being provided. In the worst examples the 'eclectic' or 'integrative' label was nothing more than a means of describing a patchwork of practices reflecting the differences among the trainers' experiences more than any coherent discipline. A CRG working party was set up to provide guidelines by which eclective or integrative courses could show their coherence in their submission document. The resulting guidelines are reproduced below.

In presenting their submission, courses are asked specifically to explain their position on the following:

1. Is the course eclectic or integrative in nature? A definition of the type or approach to eclecticism or integration being advocated is to be given in clear, non-jargon terms. If the course is eclectic, for example, how does it differentiate from an integrative rationale (and vice versa)?

   Responses to the following questions should clearly demonstrate the eclectic or integrative nature of the core theoretical model.

2. What assumptions are made about the nature and development of human beings?
3. How do psychological problems develop?
4. How does the model account for the perpetuation of psychological problems?
5. How does the model explain the process of therapeutic change?
6. What is the range of therapeutic interventions explicated in the core model?
7. What theoretical framework underpins the counselling process and range of therapeutic interventions? How does it help counsellors integrate or select interventions? Does it show how counsellors might intervene differently with different clients at different points in the counselling process?
8. How does the model deal with any apparent discrepancies between theoretical and practical aspects?
9. How does the course help students to understand the process of eclecticism and integration and learn to apply the model?
10. How do other alternative approaches or models taught on the course relate to the core eclectic or integrative model? (BAC, 1993a, pp. 1-2)

The guidelines go on to suggest the following:

a) If there are no well articulated published exemplars which deal fully with these questions, then a full description of the eclectic or integrative approach being advocated, including a detailed response to these questions, should be provided in the submission. (BAC, 1993a, p. 3)

This recommendation is to ensure that the eclectic or integrative model that underpins the course is a disciplined one and that the core staff have thought through and can articulate the relevant issues. Furthermore, a fully developed, written account of an eclectic or integrative model that has not been previously published can be made available to potential students to help them make an informed decision about applying for the course.

b) In the Visit Stage of the recognition process, Panel members will pay particular attention to the degree of congruence between tutors' ideas and students' ideas of the eclectic or integrative model in question. (BAC, 1993a, p. 3)

If students and staff have a different idea of the eclectic or integrative core model, then there is obviously something seriously wrong and either or both of the following possibilities must be considered: (a) the staff may not be teaching the model clearly enough; (b) the calibre of the students may be in doubt.

c) The eclectic or integrative core model should inform the theory, skills, supervision and client work of all students. In this respect, courses which encourage their students to develop their *own* eclectic or integrative model without being underpinned by a core theoretical model are not admissible to the scheme. (BAC, 1993a, p. 3)

While the BAC Courses Recognition Group is not against courses which encourage students to develop their own eclectic or integrative model, it cannot at present consider such courses for recognition without a core integrative framework. Remember that a defining characteristic of a professional training course is that there should be a core theoretical model which permeates the course and ensures coherence. A course which encourages students to develop their own model may, at its end, help spawn eighteen such models if there are eighteen students on the course. Courses of this nature are valuable after students have completed a professional counsellor training but should not in our opinion be undertaken until such training has been completed and students have had an opportunity to consolidate their learning. After they have done this, they will have the necessary experience to develop their own organizing frameworks if they choose to do so.

Having considered the role of the core theoretical model in professional counsellor training courses, in the next chapter we will consider the issue of the staff who teach on such courses and the resources that are needed to run them properly.

# FOUR
# Staffing and resource issues

Anyone responsible for running a course will probably be familiar with what can feel like a perennial struggle to ensure adequate staffing and resources. This chapter is in two sections. The first section examines in some detail the critical issue of staffing a counsellor training course and the second section deals more briefly with accommodation, equipment and the necessary support services.

## COURSE TEAM

Counsellor training is labour intensive. BAC-recognized courses require a core or central staff team. Central staff are defined as those who make a substantive contribution to admission, assessment, course management and decision-making, as well as teaching or supervision.

Counsellor training can be exciting and rewarding, but being involved with students trying to come to terms with the doubts and conflicts in both their personal and professional development can be demanding and emotionally draining. One implication is that courses are better run by teams rather than by individuals. It is probably fair to say that people working in a team produce courses of better quality than people working alone. Rowntree (1981) suggests that this is due in large part to the stimulus of discussion, sharing responsibilities and the need to satisfy one's peers. Courses run primarily by one person are likely to provide a more limited training experience than courses run by a staff team. Individuals who also own the premises in which they run a course as sole arbiters, accountable only to themselves, are particularly vulnerable to allegations of biased and omnipotent management and professional and ethical misconduct.

Courses 'owned' and run by one person cannot be recognized by BAC.

The minimal central team consists of two staff for a course group of about twenty students. Even then, it is unlikely that such a small team would be able to cover all elements of training adequately. High-quality training requires extensive small group work for skills development, seminars and clinical supervision, as well as one-to-one tutorials. This means that courses must have a high ratio of staff to students. One staff member to every eight to ten students would be a reasonable guideline. Staff salaries take the largest slice of the course budget and if the burden is not partially absorbed by the institution, then all of it will have to come out of the students' own pockets. Dryden and Thorne (1991, p. 13) suggest that counsellor training may already have become inaccessible to those without substantial financial resources. They lament that if this is so counselling training will undoubtedly be deprived of many potentially gifted practitioners, especially from the ethnic minority groups in this country. Although this does little to address the problem, people who have obtained places on BAC-recognized courses can apply to BAC for a bursary.

When appointing staff, courses need to pay attention to the overall profile of the staff team in terms of age, gender, race and culture. In this sense, the ideal profile would reflect that of the student group and more importantly the client population with which the students work as counsellors. The reality is that many staff teams do not reflect the student or client population. We believe that the central staff must take responsibility for initiating discussion within the course community of particular issues around power and oppression and be continually aware of the possible implications of an unrepresentative staff team. It is not enough to assume that the minority man, black or older person in the student group restores the balance or, indeed, that they will feel comfortable and not need support from staff, however vociferous their efforts to represent their minority perspective. In courses in which the staff team fully reflects the profile of the student group, yet remains unrepresentative of the client population, the danger is that the issue will be avoided and the course community seduced by the collusive ethos of shared personal characteristics. As all three authors are middle-aged men, we hesitate to draw attention to the fact that many courses have predominantly white female staff and that this reflects the prevalent white female student population.

## QUALIFICATIONS AND EXPERIENCE

The staff team must have the appropriate qualifications and experience to teach all aspects of the course programme. This does not mean that each member of staff must be qualified to teach every aspect, but recognizes that each member will make their own particular contribution. However, we do regard it as essential that the majority of core staff has at least a directly relevant and similar level of qualification to that for which the students are being trained. Staff need to be adequately trained in the core theoretical model, so for example, staff with a Psychoanalytic training would not be expected to teach Person-Centred counselling. Surprisingly, this does occasionally happen, but such courses would not be admissible to the BAC scheme for course recognition. A course which has been set up and is run by psychologists with no further counsellor training would be similarly inadmissible. The relationship between psychotherapy and counselling is, as might be expected, blurred, if not controversial. A course offered by staff trained as psychotherapists would normally be acceptable, providing the staff regarded their own psychotherapy training as both theoretically and practically consistent with counselling.

The majority of the central staff team and clinical supervisors need to be active counsellors. In BAC-recognized courses at least half the central staff must be either BAC-accredited counsellors or eligible for accreditation. This means that they are currently working with clients and have regular consultative supervision for their own counselling practice. The continuing interaction between theory and practice is of fundamental importance in counsellor training. The trainer's own work with clients provides the major stimulus for creativity and illustrative material. It is the principal source of face validity in the eyes of trainees. Staff who no longer practise will soon lose the immediacy of the experience and it is hard to maintain even an aura of competence and sustain credibility as a trainer through role or reputation alone.

Supervisors are not always members of the central staff team. Some courses either employ outside supervisors, or more frequently, require students to make their own arrangements. This raises the issue of the supervisors' knowledge of the core theoretical model taught on the course. Perhaps it is self-evident that training supervision needs to be compatible with the core training model. Certainly we believe that counsellors-in-training should receive supervision from supervisors who currently practise as counsellors or therapists. However, there is some debate about whether supervisors should be qualified and actually use the core training model in their own counselling practice or whether it is adequate that they are familiar with the model and able to provide appropriate supervision. In extreme cases it must, if nothing else, be confusing for students on, say, a Gestalt course to receive supervision from someone who is trained and practises Person-Centred counselling. We have heard that such situations do occur and find them hard to condone. Many courses provide a list of approved supervisors for students to contact. The criteria for approval would normally include relevant theoretical orientation, knowledge of the course and an agreement to adhere to the appropriate code of ethics (e.g. BAC Code of Ethics and Practice for Supervision of Counsellors).

We have already emphasized that staff need to be appropriately qualified to teach the core theoretical model and have come across courses that recruit ex-students as staff. This may be deliberate policy or just a matter of expediency but it does have the distinct advantage that staff will have had a similar training experience and are more likely to have a view of the core theoretical model consistent with that of the course. The most obvious disadvantage is the potentially incestuous party-line and therefore relatively limited ways in which staff may be able to contribute alternative perspectives and ways of working that can enrich and develop the training programme. Perhaps the answer is that courses should avoid recruiting staff entirely from ex-students. A more common difficulty is that it is the institution rather than the course that employs and therefore appoints staff. This can result in staff with often disparate theoretical backgrounds and current practice that is entirely inconsistent with the core training model. To use a musical analogy of compatibility between staff and the core training model, students may experience it as indoctrination if all staff play exactly the same tune on the same instrument, but it is important that all staff at least play the same instrument, perhaps with a different style if not a different tune.

After initial training and on-going practice for several years it can be regarded as a natural career progression to become a supervisor and then a counsellor trainer. The question is, does experience as a counsellor qualify someone to become a trainer? Do trainers need to be trained in training? Typically, the answer is that it all depends on the person. If people have experience as teachers or trainers, even in a subject not directly related to counselling, providing they are also experienced counsellors, it seems a relatively small step for them to analyse counselling in terms of knowledge and competencies and develop ways of teaching it to others. If people have no experience of teaching it seems to us essential that they enter a period of apprenticeship under the stewardship of one of the central staff. This seems to be the only option available, as at the present time there are very few courses offering training as a counsellor trainer.

## STAFF ROLES AND RESPONSIBILITIES

Staff roles and responsibilities will vary with the size of the course and the type of organization in which it is based. In most courses the key staff role is that of the course leader, who will have overall responsibility for 'making things happen'. The functions usually associated with this role include academic leadership, course management, course administration and pastoral care responsibilities. In a CNAA survey (1992, p. 3) of leaders from a diversity of courses at different phases of development, there was a remarkable degree of consensus regarding what they felt should be the major function of their job, i.e. academic leadership. The most important aspects of this function were seen as the development and implementation of the course philosophy and curriculum, quality assurance and forward planning and innovation. Despite the importance placed on these functions by the course leaders who contributed to the CNAA survey, in practice much of their time appeared to be spent on routine administrative and pastoral matters. In most cases, the course leader will be one of the main teachers or trainers on the course and will be both known to and available for consultation by all students who are taking the course. Pastoral work, which tends to revolve around giving appropriate help and advice of a personal and professional nature not only to the students, but sometimes to staff as well, can take up a considerable amount of time. It is often the case of the urgent taking priority over the important. The course leader has to respond to immediate organizational problems, such as gaining access to the teaching room or equipment needed for the next session, arranging cover for staff who are ill, and so on. They may also have to deal with a dilemma faced by an individual student before attending to other tasks. Communication with others is one of the principal aspects of course management both at the institutional level and in some cases, outside the institution. The course leader must monitor the operation of the course and report on its progress to departmental or institutional managers and committees and liaise with external examiners, professional bodies, potential sponsors of courses, potential consumers and also employers of consumers. The course leader is responsible for the recruitment and admission of students, day-to-day running of the course, student assessment and course evaluation. The course leader is also responsible for securing adequate resources and is typically the 'go-between' – that is, between the resource provider and the course. However, course leaders seldom hold the purse strings or the means of controlling resources and this lack of power can undermine their management role and make it difficult to delegate many functional tasks to other staff.

In some courses other members of the central staff team take on formal responsibility for some aspects of course organization and management. These roles typically include an admissions tutor for the course and year tutors who have responsibility for the smooth running of the programme and the related administration and pastoral care either for a particular cohort of students throughout their time on the course or for a particular year of the course. Other possible roles include academic module or unit leader and fieldwork placement co-ordinator, but it seems essential, especially with the courses that recruit a large number of students or operate two or more concurrent course groups, that some form of preferably negotiated and formal division of management functions is established.

## EXTERNAL ROLES

There are several formal roles undertaken by people external to the course. All professional training courses need to have some system of external moderation. We will deal with the appointment of examiners in some detail because, while most universities and similar institutions publish their own guidelines, the issue is not widely discussed. In most institutions the course staff will be invited to nominate people as external examiners, but they will be approved and the actual appointment will be made by the institutional management to whom the external person is accountable and from whom a fee will be received. The term of office of an external examiner is normally four years, by agreement with the individual. In order to avoid the development of a potentially collusive relationship between course staff and the external examiner with a resulting loss of impartiality, the term of office is generally only extended in special circumstances, for example in the case of a new course or in order to ensure continuity between successive external examiners and then only for a limited period. The external examiner would need to be appropriately qualified and normally have at least some previous experience of external examining or comparable experience to indicate competence in assessing students in the subject area concerned. Most institutions insist that there must not be more than one external from the same institution and that there must not be reciprocal external examining between courses or departments in two institutions. Some institutions will not appoint an external examiner who holds the position for more than one other course. Perhaps the most important condition is that the external examiner will not be influenced by any current or previous personal or professional association with the course, the staff or any of the students. The main function of the external examiner is to monitor and safeguard the standard of students' work and be able to compare the performance of students with that of their peers on comparable courses elsewhere. We will discuss the issues and identify the typical duties and responsibilities normally associated with the external examiner role in the later chapter on assessment.

Counsellor training courses may have two further external roles that are not normally associated with other courses. The first is that of course consultant. The course consultant is a consultant to the central staff team. In practice it tends to be a more informal role than that of external examiner. The person invited to be the consultant would be agreed by the staff and would usually be paid directly from the course funds, although occasionally it is possible to tap into some departmental or institutional staff development budget. The main function of the course consultant is to facilitate effective functioning of the central staff team. The course consultant has a role that Rowntree (1981) describes as 'critical friend'. He suggests that only a 'critical friend', with no personal stake in the course, can dare to confront colleagues with the tensions that may be apparent to an outsider about the way they feel about one another and quietly insist that they discuss the implications. Rowntree (1987, p. 245) describes the consultant as someone who is 'with the staff group yet not of it'. As critical friend, the course consultant can draw attention to stresses and contradictions and aspects of the course that seem not to be working well, but remain unacknowledged. The course consultant would probably be a practising counsellor with experience as a group facilitator and would preferably not have any previous or current personal or professional relationship with any member of staff. A course consultant may be brought in for a particular staff training event or agree to visit each year as part of the annual course evaluation. It is generally accepted that the external examiner and course consultant roles should not be held by the same person, indeed, published criteria for the appointment of external examiners would usually prohibit this combining of roles. However, because of the philosophy and type of assessment procedures which may be consistent with the core theoretical model, for example on a Person-Centred course, it can be argued that it is difficult to separate the roles and desirable that they should be carried out by the same person. As with many training issues, a course applying for BAC recognition would be expected to present and justify its policy. In this way, different approaches can be judged on their own merits.

The final external role is that of complaints mediator or ombudsperson. As with the external consultant, the role of complaints mediator is peculiar to counsellor training courses and is a recommendation that has come out of a review of standards and procedures on counsellor training courses carried out by BAC over the last few years. Current guidelines being produced by the BAC Courses Recognition Group suggest that the external mediator duties should be an integral part of the published complaints and appeals procedure for each course. We will discuss this in greater detail in the chapters on assessment and evaluation. BAC-recognized course partnerships may have some form of reciprocal arrangement – each course providing a named person as external mediator for the other course, but with the condition that, as with all the external roles, the person appointed would have no other associations with the institution, course staff or students that might in any way be seen as a threat to their impartial status. The external mediator would hopefully not have a regular commitment to the course, but it does mean that courses need to have a reserve budget to pay the mediator as and when the situation arises.

## STAFF MEETINGS

At the beginning of this chapter we emphasized the importance of courses being run by staff teams rather than by individuals, but this in itself makes demands on staff time and may have financial ramifications. Few counsellor trainers would argue with the need to meet regularly with others on the staff team. This is more easily achieved if staff work full-time within the institution in which the course is based, but some staff may be employed on a sessional basis, with meetings regarded as extra-curricular and unpaid commitments. The ideal scenario is for the central staff team to meet regularly each week to discuss the routine running of the course. With small teams of two or three full-time staff this may be achieved on an informal, almost *ad hoc* basis, although there is always the risk that other demands will take over and reduce staff communication to remedial or urgent matters only. With all courses, but especially those with large staff numbers that include part-time or sessional trainers, meetings should be formally scheduled preferably once every three or four months, but not less than twice each year. The effectiveness of any central staff team depends on the ability of its members to exchange ideas freely and to feel involved in the life and decisions of the team. One useful analysis of team life defines three areas of need: task, maintenance and individual needs (Verba, 1961). In the present economic climate, courses in most institutions are faced with having to 'achieve more with less'; in the case of counsellor training there is often a pressure to recruit more students, with concomitant reduction in real terms of staff resources. This situation inevitably results in pressure on staff to concentrate on who is going to do what, when, where and how, and other tasks necessary for the course to run. At first sight, it may be only these task needs which are visible and obvious, but as with an iceberg, the major areas of need in the life of a staff team may lie hidden beneath the surface. Individual staff need to feel that they belong, that they are able to contribute, that their area of expertise is respected and any individual problems are heard. The maintenance needs are concerned with the relationships among the staff and the openness and co-operation between them. It is with this aspect of staff team functioning that the external consultant can make such a valuable contribution. The strength and the continued effectiveness of the central staff team may depend on the degree to which the maintenance needs of the group and the needs of individual members are recognized and met.

## STAFF SUPPORT AND DEVELOPMENT

Trainers need to be able to allocate time for their own personal and professional development. In this respect there are obvious parallels between counselling and counsellor training. Stress and the possible consequence of what is commonly referred to as burn-out or exhaustion is now recognized as being a hazard for those employed in the helping and caring professions (Bailey, 1985). Counselling is no exception. By its very nature, counselling makes considerable emotional demands on counsellors and without adequate supervision can result in excessive stress and deterioration in standards of counselling (Dryden, 1995a). Counsellor trainers are similarly not immune to stress. The combination of overcommitment and the disparate demands of preparation and teaching, having to deal with student problems, organizational and quality assurance requirements and maintaining a client work practice, together with the time and effort associated with on-going personal and professional development, can culminate in what some trainers experience as an inexorable workload. Ironically, it can be the same sources of potential stress that make the role of trainer such an exciting and challenging one. It is possible for trainers to become tired and bored with what might feel like the repetitive nature of their work with each successive cohort of students or become complacent or indifferent about their work. As counsellors need regular supervision, trainers, too, must monitor their work and be similarly able to account to trainees and colleagues for what they do and why. Course staff have to monitor their effectiveness, resilience and be able to recognize when their personal resources are so depleted that they need to seek help (BAC, 1985). Although stress is highly individual and often a variable phenomenon, people who work as counsellor trainers might reasonably expect to have their own personal counselling at some time or at various points during their career. In some courses personal counselling for staff is regarded as a normal part of on-going self-development rather than as a response to periods of high stress. The regular meetings of the central staff team will have a supportive and developmental function, but unless there is an explicit staff support agenda, such meetings tend to be primarily task-orientated. One solution is to set up specially designated staff support groups which may from time to time involve an external facilitator.

The issues concerning staff support and staff development are closely allied with evaluation and appraisal. The BAC Code of Ethics for Trainers (BAC, 1995) states that 'trainers should arrange for regular evaluation of their work by a professional consultant or supervisor'. Most courses would at least acknowledge the potential value of an external consultant to facilitate staff team development, even if it was outside their budget for anything more than once a year. Attitudes towards staff supervision and appraisal vary – we suspect it remains a low priority for many courses pressed by demands on staff time, lack of money and other more immediate issues to do with running the course. The theoretical orientation of the course may also influence policy with regard to staff support with some courses regarding staff supervision, support and appraisal as an integral function of the staff team while others regard these as the responsibility of the course director. However, the most common practice is to regard supervision as the responsibility of the individual member of staff and something that should be undertaken by external supervisors with no feedback to the course. We do not advocate any particular approach, only that courses should have an explicit policy on staff support, supervision, appraisal and self-development.

Trainers are expected to commit themselves to undertaking further training at regular intervals and consistently to seek ways of increasing their professional development and self-awareness (BAC, 1995). In our experience most staff feel that some form of ongoing professional training not only helps to enrich their work as trainers, but helps to preserve their sanity! There are a whole variety of ways in which staff seek to extend their knowledge and experience. These typically include membership of professional bodies, participating in local branch activities, attending short courses and conferences, as well as keeping up to date with current research findings related to the core theoretical model. Staff working in universities and academic institutions will be expected to be involved with their own research and writing as part of academic development connected with their main teaching field. One of the most important dimensions of staff development is helping the trainer to extend himself or herself in the role. Hence, a trainer may be supported in taking on a new administrative or teaching responsibility, which represents for them an attainable challenge, given on-going encouragement and supervision by the course leader or other staff. This philosophy of supported staff development may also be extended to the role of *trainee trainer*, where a prospective trainer is helped to make the transition.

## RELATIONSHIPS WITH INSTITUTIONS

One of the advantages of working as a full-time member of staff on courses based in larger institutions is that staff may have access to financial support from departmental staff development budgets. Attending conferences is a typical example. Such institutions may also allocate time for staff to be involved in professional development activities as part of their normal paid contract. However, there is one exception to this. Maintaining practitioner status as an essential adjunct to teaching on professional or applied courses, such as counsellor training, is recognized only in more enlightened institutions. There is a long way to go before continuing to practise as a counsellor – and for BAC-accredited counsellors this means not less than 150 hours each year – is generally accepted, let alone actually required by institutions.

Another fairly common issue is the potential conflict of interest between, on the one hand, increased demands for value for money and greater efficiency through increasing student numbers, and on the other hand, courses that want to retain the optimum number of students for existing accommodation, facilities and staffing levels. On counselling courses the size of each student cohort will radically affect the group cohesiveness and dynamics. The course group itself remains one of the most potent and intrinsic arenas for student learning. Increasing student numbers enhances income from the course but also threatens the quality of training.

The central issue in the relationship between the course and the institution or organization revolves around collegial authority represented by committee structures and management authority as represented by directorates and senior managers. The capacity to get things done lies increasingly with the latter, but the course and more especially the course leader is part of the former and can become involved in negotiations with a complex web of organizational power and resource centres. A critical aspect is the appointment of new and appropriately qualified staff over which the course may have relatively little power to influence, especially if staff are expected to contribute to several other courses run by the institution.

Most institutions support or actively encourage the validation or recognition of their courses by professional bodies, such as the British Association for Counselling. The requirements of external recognition provide the course with a rationale and lever with which to negotiate further resources within the institution. For example, BAC-recognized courses have to maintain certain standards of staffing and accommodation if they are to retain their recognized status.

## RESOURCES

Although lack of adequate resources clearly imposes constraints on the way in which a course is run, apart from staffing, the resource requirements of counsellor training courses are modest. In this section we will comment briefly on the issues connected with accommodation, library facilities, equipment and secretarial support.

Without doubt, the most important aspect of accommodation is a base room for the course. While it may not be absolutely essential, it is certainly very desirable to have a pleasant, congenial and appropriately furnished room. Physical surroundings can have a significant impact on the quality of the learning climate and the experience students have of the course. The base room for the main course meetings and teaching sessions has to be large enough to comfortably accommodate the whole course group in an open circle or U-shaped arrangement of chairs or seats. The ideal room shape is square, but it also needs to be flat rather than a tiered lecture theatre and have some form of wall-to-wall carpeting. Carpets help to soften the noise levels that can be generated by small group experiential work – and there are occasions when counsellors in training prefer to sit or even lie on the floor! Unless other small rooms are available the type and lay-out of furniture needs to be flexible so that it is comparatively easy to switch from one-to-one, to small-group, to large-group activities. Long and narrow rooms and those with rows of desks or tables are totally unsuitable for counselling courses. In some colleges and universities in which space is at a premium and rooms are used at different times by a variety of courses, the system for room allocation may be computerized. Such systems tend to be based on student numbers and some notional optimum room capacity. They seldom take into account the nature of the course and how space might be used. It may be hard for resource managers and bureaucratic administrators, let alone our colleagues on other courses run in large multidisciplinary institutions, to understand what might seem as the idiosyncratic needs of counsellor training – that is, unless we persist in our efforts to educate them!

Courses run in private organizations established primarily to provide counsellor training courses tend not to have the problems with base rooms that exist in colleges and universities. Typically their course rooms are solely used for counsellor training and are often the envy of their colleagues in the state or public sector. With comfortable chairs or floor cushions and attractive decor it is possible to create a warm and friendly environment. This is often in stark contrast to the bare and austere public lecture rooms in some colleges and universities in which framed pictures on the walls, ornaments on shelves and large pot plants on the floor may not survive a day.

Each member of the central staff team needs an office, somewhere to attend to paperwork and conduct student tutorials in private without being disturbed. Staff offices may also be used for small supervision and seminar groups, if alternative rooms are not available.

Counselling courses first developed in university settings have tended to place strong emphasis on academic credibility and insist on what may be seen as totally unnecessary and unrealistic library provision by courses first developed outside traditional academic institutions (Dryden and Thorne, 1991). Nevertheless, academic knowledge and learning from books is an important part of counsellor training and some kind of library provision is essential. One of the advantages of courses run in traditional academic settings is that they tend to have extensive libraries stocked with books and journals that do not have to be purchased out of income from the course. Such libraries also tend to have computerized reference systems, trained library staff, and are usually open each day and sometimes at weekends. While students on counsellor training courses normally want to purchase several of the basic textbooks, it is unreasonable to ask them to have their own personal copies of all the books that they might need at one time or other on the course. Increasingly, professional counsellor training courses are being regarded as offering postgraduate or post-experience education and training. One implication for pedagogical policy is that at this level students cannot expect the whole course to be based on a single core text and need to be able to decide for themselves which books from a recommended list are most relevant to the course. It is important that both students and staff have access to a wide range of books related to each element of the course. Equally important, in order to keep up to date with current research findings and recent developments in the field, is that they have access to at least some of the relevant academic journals. Technical or scientific books and journal subscriptions are costly and the smaller and privately run courses find that this can eat away a substantial proportion of their annual budget. This is a problem for the increasing number of counselling courses run outside traditional academic settings that are currently seeking validation by universities. Another issue is that some courses, run on weekend or one-week residential blocks, are held in hired accommodation in attractive rural conference centres. The problem is where to house a library and how students, who sometimes travel long distances, are to gain access to the library other than when they attend the course. One partial solution is for the course to build up a mobile library of multiple copies of articles and key chapters (preferably made with the publishers' permission), together with one or two copies of an albeit limited range of course textbooks. This solution would be inadequate for university validation, but may satisfy student needs and, if the collection is substantial enough, the requirements for BAC course recognition.

Video recording can be a potent source of learning, especially for counselling skills training (Kagan, 1984). This is another resource aspect in which colleges and universities may have the advantage over courses run by smaller private organizations. Although they may have to plan ahead and remember to book the equipment from a central departmental pool, staff may have access to several – perhaps six or more – complete sets of video recording and playback equipment. These may be located in special laboratory or interview rooms with one-way mirrors and have the benefit of trained and readily available technical support staff. However, this remains a luxury for all but a few courses, even in the university sector. Those courses that have this type of video facility can encourage students to bring their own video tape and keep an on-going record of their skills training work, which can then be reviewed on their own VTR at home. The initial cost of video equipment imposes inevitable constraints, so most courses make do with one camera and one VTR and monitor. Certainly, the facility to at least show a video can be very useful.

The value of audio tape recording in counsellor training is now well argued (Dryden, 1993; Jacobs, 1993). The advantage of audio over video tape recording is that the cost of a small tape recorder is usually within the pocket of most students and it is easily portable for use with clients in the field and brought into the course for skills training and supervision sessions. Only a few courses have enough equipment to allow students to borrow and take it away, even for a limited period.

Another potentially valuable piece of equipment, well within the budget of most courses, is a course noticeboard. This should ideally be located adjacent to the course base room and used for standing notices such as timetables and other information about the course, opportunities for client work (increasingly circulated to courses by outside agencies) and for student notices. One warning though: noticeboards need to be regularly up-dated if they are not to be ignored!

The last but not least resource issue is the need for secretarial support. Most courses will have immediate access to a photocopier. Staff working in larger institutions will have available more sophistic-ated reprographic services for the production of student handbooks and teaching material. In large institutions with general office staff to service a variety of courses, it is all too easy to take for granted efficient typists and the qualified secretary who is able to cope with routine course administration, filing systems and telephone reception work. Without this back-up the course may slowly grind to a halt, with staff submerged in paperwork which most are not qualified or trained to handle. Indeed, any deficiency a course may have in secretarial support is likely to emerge at the earlier time of recruiting and admitting trainees. This major area of 'admission' is the focus of our next chapter.

# FIVE

# Admission

With the staffing and other resources in place the course is ready to admit students. The term 'admission' encompasses a number of activities from the time the new course is publicized, through selection and on to the reception of students on to the course.

The success of the admission procedures might be measured by the student drop-out rate later in the course because the aim of admission is to help the course and the students to assess the degree of fit between the training offered and the readiness of the student to make use of that training. An effective admission process will yield a full student cohort ready at the outset to make maximum use of the training. An ineffective admission process yields misinformed and sometimes aggrieved students not to mention a stressed staff trying to deal with the gulf between the students' wishes and potentialities and what the course can provide.

## PUBLICIZING THE COURSE

Publicity can be relatively expensive but the most powerful form, word-of-mouth publicity, costs absolutely nothing. Word-of-mouth publicity involves current or former course members and their friends communicating fact and opinion about the course to potential applicants. Word-of-mouth publicity is not so relevant to the selection of a first cohort of students except that the course will already be beginning to build up some kind of reputation by the way it presents itself to early enquirers. It is also important for the course to remember that word-of-mouth publicity can be powerfully negative as well as positive. Here we recall a course which began about a year before it was ready. Although the first run of the course had a full cohort of students the subsequent negative word-of-mouth publicity led to it failing to recruit a second cohort.

Some successful courses rely entirely on inexpensive word-of-mouth publicity but in doing so they run a danger of becoming too homogeneous, depending as they do on word spreading within the limited circles of their previous students. A counselling training course would prefer to be fairly heterogeneous so that, in working with each other, the students are able to share a range of previous experiences, cultures and values, making it a rich and challenging interpersonal experience.

Arriving at a heterogeneous cohort of students involves gaining visibility for the course in a variety of circles. This may be achieved through directing advertising at designated groups of people. For example, the professional journals and magazines within counselling offer access to a reliably appropriate readership at reasonable cost. Advertising in national newspapers is considerably more expensive though it does reach more people. However, national newspaper advertising, compared to journal advertising, tends to result in a large proportion of enquiries from people for whom counselling training is not appropriate at that time. The course must be prepared to respond to these initial enquiries with very detailed information and guidance lest the course be inundated with inappropriate applications which can take up much staff time and result in applicants feeling disappointed and rejected.

Courses seeking to maintain a level of heterogeneity might target specific populations, for example, international students and students from minority groups. This requires considerable investigation of the chosen populations in order to find entry points for publicity. For example, while the *Guardian* is a recognized location for national advertising, the course interested in attracting international students might be more drawn to the *Guardian Weekly*, which has an international circulation.

Another way in which a course can effectively publicize itself is through the profile which it establishes within the community. Activities such as delivering public lectures and workshops, assisting voluntary counselling agencies, offering a free public counselling service and giving an unbiased consultation service to public enquiries about training all contribute to the financial costs rather than the profits of a training establishment. However, all of these activities will be contributing positively to the publicizing of the training institution by maintaining its profile within the community. The public are appreciative of such help freely and willingly offered, though courses should be aware that it can be an enormous drain on resources. For example, the training unit run by one of the authors deals with about 2,000 enquiries a year about counselling and counselling training. Each of these enquiries represents a person with unique circumstances and requires an individual response.

## INFORMATION PROVIDED TO PROSPECTIVE APPLICANTS

A proportion of the enquiries from the public will be from prospective applicants to the course. Responding to these enquiries is most effectively achieved through producing a detailed course booklet. There is some advantage in making this booklet fairly comprehensive because the more questions which it answers then the more staff time will be saved handling subsequent enquiries. A typical booklet of this kind might deal with issues such as the following:

- details on the training establishment
- the history of the training course
- the core theoretical model of the course
- the aims of the course
- the structure of the course
- course content
- criteria for on-going counselling practice
- supervision
- assessment details
- criteria for course completion
- course fees and all additional costs
- selection criteria and procedure
- details on the likely membership of the course
- how to obtain an application form
- preparatory work for the course
- details on the staff.

Prospective students are discerning readers when it comes to a comparison of course booklets. There is a general frustration felt about booklets which do not give a detailed picture of *all* the costs of undertaking the training including not only the tuition fees but also the more hidden costs, such as perhaps external individual supervision, personal therapy, plus any travel and accommodation which may be required for residential elements.

Readers make judgements about the quality of a course from its course booklet, in particular the coherence with which the core model and content is described and also the information given on staff. It is surprising how many course booklets give little or no detail on the most important resource provided, namely the staff personnel. It is reasonable to suggest that essentially the depth of the course is defined by the depth of training, development and experience of its staff.

Increasingly, course booklets are including some statement about the position of the training course with respect to equal opportunities. Often this is nothing more than a somewhat condescending sounding list of groups in relation to which the course affirms its lack of prejudice. It might be more helpful to the prospective applicant from a minority group to get more information and a positive statement about the course's position. For example, simply stating that the course does not seek to prejudice students in relation to the issue of sexual orientation is not particularly reassuring for the gay student who is used to institutionalized prejudice hiding behind blind unawareness. The student might be more confident that the relevant issues had been considered if the course clearly stated that its core theoretical model did not pathologize homosexuality. The student might be even more impressed by a course which was able to announce that it was gay affirmative because any such assertion carries considerable policy and practice implications.

Courses also need to be aware of what they are promising if they represent themselves as having an equal opportunities policy with respect to an issue such as disability. Usually this information is framed in a guarded way such as 'every effort will be made to cope with physical disability'. This statement does not represent an equal opportunities policy but simply expresses an intention to offer special assistance if that can be accommodated by existing resources. This point is sharpened if we consider the implications of accepting a deaf applicant on to a course. If that person was particularly proficient at lip-reading he or she might be able to manage some of the very small group work, but meetings of any size would require a sign language interpreter. The costs of providing that professional help are greater than may first appear because to cover sessions of any length interpreters need to work in pairs.

As well as providing written information to prospective students in the form of a booklet, courses will also be subject to further queries from prospective applicants. The two further questions most often asked are: 'How might I obtain financial help to do this training?' and 'What are the prospects for a career in counselling?'

Courses might consider producing an information sheet on the first of these questions, including details on the following:

- the policy of the local education authority on the awarding of educational grants;
- whether the course meets the criteria for the award of student loans;
- whether the course meets the criteria for the award of career development loans;
- the addresses of charitable trusts which offer financial help for counselling training;
- details of reference texts and databases listing charitable trusts.

Students might be warned that grant- or scholarship-awarding bodies vary widely in their criteria for judging applicants and courses. For example, the British Association for Counselling has a very small scholarship fund which is only open to students of its recognized courses, while the Carnegie Trust is useful in that it offers financial help to students who are not eligible for mainstream local authority grants, but other criteria apply with the training required to be full-time and at postgraduate level, not to mention the fact that the applicant must be Scottish. In general, it is easier for students of full-time courses to obtain financial help in the form of grants or loans but it is still not an easy matter and prospective students might be warned of the amount of work they will have to invest in obtaining finance, an effort that might still end in disappointment.

The second question which prospective students often pose is on the prospects for a career in counselling. In general, the degree of attractiveness of work in counselling is inversely proportional to the opportunities for such work. Many such enquiries come from workers who have already become dissatisfied as employees of statutory helping agencies. For example, counselling may appear to offer disillusioned social workers the very work context which had originally motivated them towards social work as a career. However, it is important to warn such prospective students about the difficulty of obtaining professional posts in counselling which would replace an existing salary. Although the profession of counselling is growing rapidly, there are still relatively few full-time posts and many of these are naïvely offered to social workers untrained in counselling because the former profession has historically been linked in the public eye to counselling. Although it is appropriate to forewarn students lest they be disappointed after training, it is still relevant to acknowledge that although there is no regular career structure for counsellors, the work *is* generally regarded by graduates as intrinsically satisfying and there is an increasing number of opportunities, especially for part-time and sessional work.

## THE APPLICATION PROCESS

Selection is a two-way process, in which both parties are seeking to achieve the same thing: to judge the degree of fit between the applicant and the course. If either party makes the wrong selection decision then the result will prove inefficient for both. Since selection is a co-operative venture an important first step for the course is to be explicit about the selection criteria which they will be employing so that both applicant and course can work towards the same end.

### Selection criteria

The guidelines for selection criteria relevant to BAC-recognized courses are understandably general and loosely defined. It would not be appropriate for such national guidelines to be too prescriptive since courses emanate from a wide range of educational institutions, all of which will have their own requirements with respect to selection criteria. Instead, the BAC course recognition guidelines emphasize the personal dimensions of the successful applicant:

> Those selected should show evidence of the following attributes or the potential for developing them:
>
> - self-awareness, maturity and stability;
> - ability to make use of and reflect upon life experience;
> - capacity to cope with the emotional demands of the course;
> - ability to cope with the intellectual and academic requirements;
> - ability to form a helping relationship;
> - ability to be self-critical and use both positive and negative feedback;
> - some awareness of the nature of prejudice and oppression of minority groups.
>
> Selectors should seek evidence that an applicant's primary need is not for personal therapy or personal growth. (BAC, 1990, p. 4)

On their own initiative, BAC-recognized courses have gone further in specifying appropriate selection criteria. The following questions illustrate the most commonly applied criteria. Not every course would hold to all these criteria and courses would vary with respect to those criteria held to be of paramount importance. Each of these criterion questions is presented with a brief discussion.

*Does the applicant have prior counselling experience?* Prior counselling experience makes selectors feel more confident that the applicant has tested himself or herself in counselling contexts and is confident that the role is right for them. It is rare to take people on lengthy counselling training without such previous counselling experience.

*Does the applicant have previous experience, as a client, of counselling or therapy?* Some courses will require the applicant to have completed a specified minimum period of personal therapy while other courses might view this criterion less stringently, regarding such previous experience in the role of client as useful but not essential.

*Does the applicant have prior experience of counselling, or counselling skills, training?* Once again, courses will vary as to their requirements with respect to this criterion. Some courses may even define a particular level of prior training or indeed will prescribe a specific course which must be completed before the start of the main training. For example, a diploma course might require completion of a 120-hour certificate in counselling skills before embarking on diploma training. Other courses might regard such prior training as a useful guide as to whether the applicant has made an informed decision but may not *require* such training.

*Is the applicant more interested in counselling training as a means of personal growth or does she/he seriously want to enter the profession?* For recognized courses this is a critical selection issue. While personal growth is an integral part of counsellor training, selection endeavours to ensure that it is not the principal motivation of the applicant. The reason for the hard line taken on this criterion is that counselling training is wary of being viewed as simply providing growth experiences for rather expensive fees.

*Will the applicant be able to meet the academic challenges involved in the course?* Some courses will be required to lay down a firm criterion regarding prior academic achievement. For example, a university-based postgraduate diploma in counselling will be required to ensure that all applicants have a prior degree or a degree equivalent. In recent years, even in university circles, this criterion for prior academic achievement is being regarded more flexibly. Sometimes university departments will be able to satisfy this requirement by taking into account the prior work experience of the applicant. The counselling profession is fortunate indeed that this flexibility has developed because there is no substantive counselling research which supports the view that a prior university degree in an unrelated subject correlates with greater effectiveness among counselling diplomates.

*Is the course coming at the right time in the applicant's development as a counsellor?* This question describes the criterion which is most responsible for failure in selection for counselling training. One of the reasons for the power of this criterion is that it is difficult for applicants to make a sound decision on their readiness without the aid of an interview or pre-interview meeting. Counselling course staff are rightly concerned that the applicant should be sufficiently developed in relation to counselling and his or her own personal growth to make optimal use of the counselling training. If applicants are too inexperienced in relation to their own personal growth and basic counselling skills it tends to take considerable time for them to engage fully, in a non-defensive way, in counselling training. Although more rare, it is also possible to find applicants who feel *too* developed already as counsellors to make full use of the training. Some counsellors who have been working for many years, yet without thorough training, find it difficult to open themselves to look critically at their current practice and take on board the ideas of training. Selectors are alive to the danger of applicants who cannot allow themselves to become 'learners'.

*Is the applicant too old or too young for training?* This can be a highly contentious criterion, particularly where courses draw rigid age guidelines, sometimes excluding applications from people under 24 years of age or over 50 years of age. The younger age limit is more common, with courses believing that people under 24 years of age are unlikely to have had sufficient life experience or personal growth to be able to engage without fear in the personal growth dimensions of the training. It is less common for courses to be explicit about an elder age limit, mainly because accusations of 'ageism' more often relate to elder limits. However, some courses will have implicit prejudices as far as age is concerned, perhaps feeling that the development of their approach will not be advanced sufficiently by training an older person who is likely to have less opportunity to develop the approach after training. When considering whether an applicant is too young or too old, actual chronological age is a somewhat weak predictor. Many courses would prefer to interview the applicant in order to make a decision on whether that person has had insufficient life experience or personal growth, or, in the case of older applicants, whether they are still open to development with respect to counselling skills and their own growth. The experience of the authors goes against specifying precise ages for this criterion since a few of the most suitable applicants they have encountered have been in their early twenties and mid-sixties while some in their thirties have seemed either far too young or far too old.

*Does the applicant have a basic awareness of, and compatibility with, the core theoretical model of the course?* The mainstream counselling approaches do not seem to differ significantly in their effectiveness (Bergin and Garfield, 1994), yet it does seem to be important that the practitioner has a coherent approach (Smith, Glass and Miller, 1980). This coherence between the counsellor and the approach is correctly emphasized in selection. Indeed, one of the strongest features of counsellor training is the willingness of training establishments to refer applicants to each other according to the perceived 'fit' between the applicant's preferences and interests and the core theoretical model of the training. If an applicant for a Person-Centred course is clearly fascinated by Psychodynamic concepts and procedures then it is appropriate he or she be referred to an equivalent Psychodynamic training so as to maximize the benefits of the integration between his or her preferences and the core theoretical model. Training courses which ignored that fit would be doing the applicant a disservice to select him or her for training in an inappropriate core theoretical model.

*Does the applicant have a personality which is inappropriate for counselling?* This is undoubtedly the most difficult selection criterion, yet one which would be held to be important by all trainers with integrity. It is appropriate that counselling trainees fall within the 'normal' range with respect to psychopathological disorders. Hopefully that normal range is not drawn unduly narrowly since any profession needs a little variability to stimulate development. However, any extreme pathology is something which selectors would wish to filter out, although, in practice, it is difficult to diagnose such pathology during selection. Psychological tests may be useful in screening for extreme psychotic or neurotic behaviour but will be much less powerful in identifying 'borderline' characteristics or personality disorder. Indeed, the activity of counselling could be particularly attractive to the 'borderline' individual who might also seem very plausible during selection. Training courses will have this criterion in mind during selection, but it is not uncommon to find errors made which are only too apparent in the early stages of training.

## The application form

Higher education institutions may have a standard application form, but for counselling courses this generally needs to be supplemented with questions relating to some of the aforementioned selection criteria. Where the course director has the authority to design the form, it is good practice to ask only those biographical questions which are really necessary. For example, if age is not a selection criterion either for the institution or for the course then there is no reason to request it.

Open-ended questions can be particularly productive in counsellor training application forms. These not only give applicants wide scope to describe themselves but offer a focusing exercise through which to explore their readiness for training. It is common for applicants to find that the process of completing the open-ended sections helps them to discover that this is not the right time to embark on such training. Sometimes an applicant even telephones or writes to the course to thank them for the process which the application form created. The sample open-ended questions listed below might each be followed by a half page or whole page left blank for the applicant's response.

- Please describe in detail your current opportunities for practising as a counsellor [if you do not have such current opportunities for practice, please give details of your plans for the nature and location of these opportunities and describe any earlier practice opportunities you may have had].
- Please describe your own view of your present strengths and weaknesses in the role of helper.
- Please discuss your reasons for wanting to embark on this course at this time in your life.
- Please go into details on the ways in which the core theoretical model of the course, as you currently understand it, relates to

your own personality and experience [do not hesitate to comment on the 'conflict' as well as the 'fit'].

- Please give your thoughts about the financial and time commitments of the course in relation to your current life.
- What makes you confident about being able to cope with the extensive reading and writing work of the course?
- Describe your earlier, or current, experience as a client both in terms of the amount of that experience and in its influence upon your decision to apply for this training.
- Please use this space to write anything else which you would want us to know about you.

## References

Requiring references is a convention which applies in all academic circles. Yet, like the emperor's new clothes, it is one which might well be questioned if its value is purely to be seen in terms of the information which it provides selectors.

It is rare for references to express a negative recommendation. Indeed, some referees acquire a distinctive reputation because they *are* willing to voice the negative as well as the positive. In such cases their positive recommendations add value to the application.

Occasionally a reference will include a negative comment or an expressed uncertainty in relation to a particular area within the application. For example, the referee might express an uncertainty about the suitability of the applicant with respect to the core theoretical model, perhaps even implying that the applicant is not particularly interested in that model but is valuing the final award or the BAC course recognition status of the training. Although the course would be grateful to this referee for his or her frankness, this intelligence is actually quite difficult to handle in the remainder of the selection process. Certainly, the selectors are now able to address that specific question of the 'fit' between the applicant and the core theoretical model of the course but it is highly questionable whether they are able to discuss openly the referee's opinion, given what is generally presumed to be a confidential reference, unless the organization has an open file policy and this has been made explicit to the referee. Nevertheless, it is useful to receive such frank opinions so that the particular area, if not the referee's opinion, can receive full attention during the interview and other selection procedures.

Rather than despair about what can sometimes feel like a meaningless convention because of the relative lack of influence of the reference upon the selection process, a training course might seek to maximize the secondary benefit of the reference procedure. It is possible to use that procedure to encourage the applicant's *consultation* with the referee(s). It can be extremely useful if the applicant is put into a position where they have to consult one or more relevant professionals about their prospective application to counselling training. A course can facilitate that consultation process by requiring the course member to engage in specific discussion with the referee prior to a reference being submitted. Such a procedure would include with the application form an information sheet for referees asking them to address specific questions, following discussion with the course applicant. Although this consultation may represent a secondary gain as far as the reference process is concerned, it adds to the spirit of open consultation and discussion that characterizes selection for counselling training. Essentially, the process is furthered if the applicants can be helped to focus as fully as possible on the appropriateness of their application at that time.

## Pre-interview consultations

As well as consulting with their referee, prospective applicants might seek a meeting with one of the course staff prior to tendering an application. Sensibly the prospective applicant may simply be wishing to meet one of the staff not only to have questions answered but also to get a sense of what it would be like to relate to that staff member as a student. These meetings are particularly useful in helping the student in his or her selection of the course, with questions flowing more easily than they do in formal interviews.

The BAC course recognition guidelines recommend that courses should involve current or former students in consultations with prospective students. It can be difficult to organize these consultations to take place at interview time since staff are often interviewing during student vacations but the effort to organize them is highly worthwhile since applicants generally ask many more questions of current students than they do of staff in the formal interview. These informal meetings or telephone conversations are usually valued equally by the current students, who enjoy reflecting on their own training and offering a service to others. It is, of course, important that the content of these consultations be kept separate from the selection decision.

## The interview

While a certificate-level course may or may not have a selection interview, more intensive recognition-level courses *must* include an interview in selection. Furthermore, that interview should create the possibility for assessment by at least two of the core staff, through either two single interviews or one interview involving two staff.

Courses will vary in the extent to which they rely on paper selection, screening out some applicants who will be declined a place without interview. Usually this paper selection is restricted to the mandatory selection criteria, only rejecting candidates who do not meet these clearly stated compulsory criteria, such as that of having prior counselling experience or a level of academic background that is suitable to postgraduate study. On those criteria which do not have such clearly specified mandatory limits it is difficult to make finer judgements only on the basis of the application form, hence the interview becomes crucial in selection.

Although applicants may be declined without an interview, it is unusual to offer a place without an interview. Indeed, recognized courses would be expected to conduct an interview even with the most attractive applicant on paper. The reason for this is that the interview is a two-way process: it is important that the applicant makes an informed decision rather than simply grasps the offered opportunity without the consultation available in an interview. In any case, courses would likely be wary of taking someone onto a recognition-level training which involves considerable personal work without having any contact with the applicant who, for all his or her prior qualifications, might prove to be unsuitable on a personal level.

It is an open question whether applicants should be expected to *pay* for their selection interview. Certainly, even a simple one-hour interview with two staff is an expensive item as far as the course is concerned, taking into consideration not only the interview but the prior meeting to discuss eligibility and the subsequent discussion on whether to offer the applicant a place, not to mention the administration involved. Probably the selection process for each applicant to a recognized counselling course costs the course something in the region of £100. Whether directly or indirectly, students are paying for this selection process. If there is no selection fee then these costs are being shared only by the successful applicants, whereas if there is a fee the costs are being shared by all applicants. Looking at it this way, it is probably fairer and more direct to charge an application fee, yet this practice is not widespread and would even be regarded as unethical in some institutions. It would be interesting to run a comparison of one condition against the other: perhaps applicants would feel empowered to take more responsibility in the process if they were paying some or all of the costs.

Selection interview decisions may be *competitive* or *individualized*. In competitive interviews the interviewee is being compared with others and places offered to those who seem to be the strongest candidates. In this condition the selection question is: 'Is there less uncertainty about this applicant than other applicants?'

In individualized interviews there is a place potentially available for each interviewee, who is then judged on his or her own merits and a place awarded if they are found suitable. In this condition the selection question is: 'Would this applicant be able to make sufficient use of the training at this time?'

The first condition allows the course to select the best prospects from those students who have applied but may prejudice the chances of the student who is suitable for training but not as good as some other applicants. The second condition is probably better for the individual student, who can be assured that any offer of a place is being judged on an individual basis, but this procedure is likely to lead to the course being filled before other, highly suitable, later applicants can be considered.

The interview, like the whole selection procedure, is concerned with clarifying the student's readiness for training at that time and also giving the student more information about the course. The more the interview can become a shared exploration of these dual purposes, the better. However, there is a tendency for interviews to become skewed towards the course's decision rather than the applicant's decision. This skewing sometimes happens for the understandable reason that the applicant has made many of his or her enquiries through previous meetings with staff and current students of the course.

The difficulty for the staff is in making judgements about personal qualities since nervousness and fear may inhibit the applicant's functioning. For example, the applicant may appear somewhat blocked or cut off from his or her feelings but it is difficult for interviewers to judge whether this is indicative of a general problem, which would make training difficult, or whether it is simply a result of the tension within the interview. Early, open-ended questions tend to ease that tension in that the interviewee gets an opportunity to represent himself or herself freely and without being over-constrained by more closed questions. Nevertheless, although making some judgements about personality is vital for the interviewers, it is difficult to believe that the interview offers a reliable method.

A number of the issues which will be raised in the interview are introduced more for the benefit of the interviewee than as part of the selection decision of the interviewers. For example, interviewers will feel some responsibility to explore the question of the amount of space the applicant has in his or her life to embark on this training course. This is not so relevant in recruitment for full-time counselling training, but many counselling courses are conducted on a part-time basis and there is a widespread tendency among students to underestimate the amount of work, which extends far beyond the actual contract hours of the course to include considerable counselling practice and supervision, not to mention extensive reading and writing. It is appropriate for the selectors to explore what space the student is able to clear in his or her life but it is also important for them to retain the perspective that their job in this regard is to help the student to become as fully aware as possible of the demands of the course while he or she still has the power to make up his or her own mind on whether they can meet those demands. Most particularly, selectors must be wary of sexism creeping into their questioning. For example, it may be relevant for selectors to help the applicant to explore childcare arrangements which will ease participation in the course, but it is not acceptable for selectors to restrict that line of questioning to female applicants and to ignore it for males.

Similarly, it is relevant for the selectors to help the applicant to identify any special needs which they may have, related to a particular disability. Open exploration of such special needs is important so that the course can become forewarned of particular preparations which it must make for an individual student. For example, special individual reading and taping may be required for a dyslexic student, depending on the student's degree of difficulty. It is also important to discover special needs which the course feels it cannot meet. For example, it is expected that recognized courses would be able to offer disabled access, but if a course cannot offer that facility for the particular disablement of the applicant it is vital that is determined in advance. It is also important that core staff have information on special needs in preparation for the beginning of the training. Students with special needs tend to value that careful preparation because they are only too familiar with neglect and omission.

Another issue frequently raised in selection interviews, not as a criterion for the selectors but as a consideration for the applicant, is the possibility that counsellor training can create disruption in the student's personal and social life. Some courses refer to this as the 'government health warning', making sure that some mention of it is made in every selection interview. The issue here is that counsellor training involves such intensive personal work in what may at times be an intimate learning context with other students that the student quickly finds that his or her personal growth is advancing much faster than that of their partner or family. It is appropriate for selectors to endeavour to warn students about that possibility, thus enabling and encouraging them to discuss it in advance with their partner or, at least, to be alive to the process as early as possible. Many applicants have already been involved in counselling training of one kind or another and are familiar with the kind of pressure it can place upon relationships. However, other applicants may be so unfamiliar with the context that the warning provided by selectors appears as a somewhat incomprehensible jumble of words. Nevertheless, students might remember the warning once the process starts. Once again, it is ethically important for selectors to emphasize to the applicant that any such 'health warning' is a matter of private consideration for the applicant and not a selection criterion for the course.

Interviewers might consider, as a matter of equal opportunities, maintaining a checklist of issues which they would want to cover in *every* interview. Such a checklist might include the following items:

- discussing the applicant's opportunities for concurrent counselling practice;
- discussing the criterion for external individual supervision;
- discussing any requirement there may be for ongoing personal therapy;
- discussing the attendance criterion;
- detailing the assessment regime;
- checking the applicant's understanding of the schedule for fee payments;
- ensuring that the applicant has an understanding of the requirements for private study;
- giving the 'health warning';
- helping the applicant to consider the space he or she will need to make in his/her life in order to cope with the demands of the course.

## ADDITIONAL SELECTION METHODS

While the application form, references and interview will be part of all selection procedures, there are some additional methods employed by individual courses. For example, the applicant may be asked to submit *essays* on specified topics. The aim here may be to ensure graduate level entry or, even with existing graduates, to test their ability with respect to psychological or counselling theory. One Masters course invites applicants to select a mainstream counselling approach and produce an essay outlining the concept which the approach has of the person, the ways in which it defines maladjustment and its conceptualization of the process of change. Applicants might expect to engage in further discussion on their essays during interview.

A fairly common additional selection method is to put a few applicants together for a leaderless *group discussion* task, often with no prescribed subject for discussion. It is unusual for courses to be explicit about their selection criteria with respect to these groups but it is a way of seeing how individuals handle this difficult interpersonal situation, perhaps relating freely and openly with each other or, on the other hand, displaying a tendency to become disabled by transference phenomena and interpersonal game-playing. The session may usefully include a final 'process review', in which participants talk about their experiences in the earlier discussion and the reasons they acted as they did. As well as giving the selectors further information, this process review may serve the function of helping participants to process the experience and leave it behind. It must be said that applicants often find that these group discussion tasks are more intimidating than an interview, perhaps because of the lack of specification of criteria.

*Personality tests* are used in numerous selection procedures but surprisingly rarely for counsellor training. We might have imagined that since counselling is so intimately related to psychology that the use of personality tests would be well developed. Furthermore, most counselling approaches place great emphasis on the personality of the counsellor as absolutely central to the counselling process. Despite the fact that embryonic attitude scales (for example, Nelson-Jones, 1982) have been available for many years, they have not been systematically used in selection. Perhaps counsellor trainers are somewhat cynical about the validity and reliability of paper and pencil tests of personality.

An additional selection method which has face validity is a *counselling skills test*, involving the applicant in a videotaped interview with a role-playing 'client'. As well as assessing the level of skill of the applicant in this interview, the videotape can be replayed with the applicant giving commentary and analysis on his or her performance. This is a highly demanding selection method – indeed exactly the same procedure is used as a *final* examination on several BAC-recognized courses. However, the method, although time-consuming, is particularly relevant for the recruitment of participants to post-diploma training, for which a high level of entry skill needs to be presumed.

## DECISION-MAKING AND FEEDBACK

Notwithstanding the decision made by the applicant following the selection process, the course will come to its conclusion as to whether he or she should be offered a place or not. Although this might be a straightforward offer or rejection intermediate decisions also are possible.

In the case of a straightforward offer of a place the course may still choose to give additional feedback to the applicant on how they were experienced during selection. Although such feedback is relatively rare and more expensive in staff time, it does represent a more personal response to a successful applicant than a simple letter offering a place.

When a place is offered the student may be given a time-limit for his or her decision, or the course may also request a deposit upon acceptance of an offer. Where a deposit is required courses customarily give more time to the applicant to make his or her decision, recognizing that the applicant needs to be fairly sure that he or she can sustain the financial and time commitments of the course before risking what is usually a non-refundable deposit. The payment of a deposit is a powerful way of inviting the applicant to focus on whether or not they want to undertake the course. This is important both for the applicant and also for the training course since counselling courses are generally not buffered financially by the state but are required to cover their costs in full. Courses which require a deposit can be fairly sure that 90 per cent of deposit-paying applicants will start the course, whereas a trainer in one university which prohibited the levying of deposits found that 60 per cent of his course withdrew in July and August before an October start! Although deposits may officially be 'non-refundable', there is usually an informal policy of refunding deposits where a replacement student is found to fill the place.

Sometimes the offer of a place is not straightforward but carries specified *conditions*. For example, if there is uncertainty even after interview as to the equivalence of the applicant's educational background to graduate entry, he or she may be asked to submit an *essay* along the lines described earlier. In some universities a normal condition in the selection of overseas students who do not already have English language certificates is completion of a *language test*. Although counselling trainers may feel somewhat uneasy about requiring such a test, they would want to find some way of ensuring that the applicant had a fairly sophisticated command of language because the practical counselling work which the student will be doing with real clients is hugely demanding of language. It must be said that conventional language tests do not sufficiently tap the areas of affective and metaphorical language which would be required in counselling practice. Perhaps an interesting research and development task for the future is to devise an appropriate test.

Another condition which may be attached to the offer of a place is that the applicant *completes a current course* before embarking upon diploma training. Since selection may be taking place from nine months to fifteen months before the commencement of the course, it is not unusual for the applicant to be in the middle of a prior certificate course. In this situation the selectors might not simply judge the applicant on present ability but make allowances for his or her development during the remainder of that current course. In this circumstance it is likely that the selectors will offer a place on condition that the applicant satisfactorily completes the current training.

Perhaps one of the most challenging 'conditions' which selectors might present to the applicant is their own *uncertainty* about the selection decision. In any educational selection procedure there is an honourable tendency to give the benefit of the doubt to the applicant. In counselling training, which tends to value dialogue, a course may openly present the applicant with the detail of their uncertainty, asking him or her to consider the issues involved and come to his or her own decision. For example, the selectors might write to an applicant:

We were not sure that this course is coming at the right time in your development as a counsellor – we thought that it is perhaps a little early and that it might be better for you to have more experience in your voluntary counselling work. However, our uncertainty is not so strong that we want to deny you a place, instead, we would like to ask you to consider the question and be assured that a place is available for you on this course and also on the subsequent course if you so wish.

In many academic circles the above letter might be decried as 'passing the buck' but it is a relevant part of the selection process in counselling, which recognizes that the other person has power to make judgements about himself or herself and in many instances can make more accurate judgements than outside persons. At the very least this invitation to the applicant to reflect upon self and come to a decision will be exercising her or his autonomy and responsibility even before the course commences.

Where the selection decision is *not* to offer the applicant a place, the question arises about how much feedback to give. Policies in this regard vary enormously, with some courses giving the applicant a one-line rejection letter and others offering two pages detailing the reasons for the decision. Some courses will even offer follow-up telephone conversations or meetings, feeling that the course has some responsibility to help the applicant to understand and cope with the decision.

Detailed feedback on why their application has been rejected is welcomed by most applicants for a number of reasons. It can help unsuccessful applicants to reorient and become better prepared for subsequent selection procedures; it can help them to understand what they might do to become acceptable for training; and in some cases the detailed feedback gives them a focus for their anger and a means of rationalizing the feeling of rejection.

As far as the course is concerned one of the most common reasons for rejecting applications is that, in the opinion of the selectors, they are not so strong as other applications and, although such decisions can be highly subjective, there are only a limited number of places on each course. Another reason is that the applicant is deemed to be 'not yet ready' for training at that level. In such cases there is strong argument for detailing that fact and giving guidance on how the applicant might become ready. In a minority of cases the rejection emanates from the selectors' uneasiness about the suitability of the personality of the applicant to counselling. Here we might consider that the selectors, who also have a responsibility to the counselling profession, might feel some obligation to make their views known to the applicant. However, selectors might also wish to consult administrators in their institution to ensure that phraseology like the following does not encourage litigation from the applicant:

Our central reason for deciding not to offer you a place was the strong uncertainty which we felt about your current suitability for counselling work. We were uneasy about the way you handled your power in relation to your current voluntary counselling which you described during interview. While this may be experienced in a positive way by your clients, as you suggested during interview, we were fearful that it could be highly disempowering for clients whether now or in the future. As well as coming to the decision not to offer you a place we also feel obliged to ask you to increase the amount of supervision you receive from your current level of one and a half hours per term and, as a matter of urgency, to discuss your current client work with your supervisor.

## INDUCTION INTO THE COURSE

The period after selection, but before the start of the course, can be used to great effect since this is a point when motivation is generally high and pre-course tasks may be undertaken with enthusiasm. Students may have several months or even a year in which to embark upon a scheme of guided reading and writing. For example, students may be invited to produce reviews of selected key texts and these reviews used early in the training in small 'study groups' or the like.

Another pre-course writing task which can help students to become 'primed' for the training is to produce autobiographies detailing the events and processes which have led them to become the people they now are. Only when the students are actually engaged on this task do they appreciate how much of a 'focusing' exercise it can be. Indeed, one student wrote at length to his trainers thanking them for this pre-course exercise and detailing how it had helped him to realize that his decision to do the training was a mistake!

A course may also endeavour to introduce the students to each other even before the course commences. At its simplest level this might take the form of circulating a participant address list, perhaps with a note encouraging contact among those who might wish to consider sharing transport, or even accommodation in the case of full-time course students coming from afar. Another way of facilitating introductions is to invite students to write half a page about themselves and send that to the course for collation and distribution around the whole student group. In courses where the students are fairly local to the training establishment, a social gathering may even be arranged some weeks before the start of training. All these pre-course procedures involve a fair amount of administrative work for the trainers but they are usually well received by participants and help considerably the establishment of early safety and trust.

Whether prior to the course or at the beginning of the training it is important to give the students detailed information on how the course will operate. This commonly would take the form of a 'course handbook for students' including such headings as the following:

The history of the course
The core theoretical model
The structure of the course
Approach to: Self-development
     Client work
     Supervision
     Skills training
     Theory
     Assessment details
     Progress regulations
     The staff and their contributions.

Having selected a cohort of students and helped them to enter the course, the main ingredients of the training may now follow. The first of these which we shall explore is the theory work of the course.

# SIX

# Theory

Theory is implicit in counselling, even though it may not be plainly apparent or expressed. Lebow (1987) argues that any approach to counselling must be underpinned by a clear and internally consistent theoretical base. We believe that if counsellors set themselves up to intervene in the lives of others, then, whatever their theoretical orientation, they should be able, at least on reflection, to account to themselves, their colleagues and their clients for what they are trying to do and why they are doing it. In Chapter 3 we discussed why initial counsellor training should be based on a clearly articulated 'core theoretical model', what the elements of such a core model should be and how the model would permeate the course. The core model is the main theory element in counsellor training, but by no means the only one.

We start this chapter by discussing the process of learning a core model of counselling. We then go on to examine briefly what we regard as the other essential theoretical elements of an in-depth professional counsellor training programme. In the final section of the chapter we say something about approaches to learning and teaching theory.

## THE PROCESS OF LEARNING A CORE MODEL

Chapter 3 explored the theory curriculum of a core model on a training course and how that core model would permeate all the facets of the course. In this section we shall explore the process for students of learning a core model.

Perhaps the initial phase of learning may be characterized by the Gestalt mechanism of introjection: the unquestioning acceptance of the major concepts and assumptions that underpin the core model. Certainly students need to grasp the essence of the model before they can begin to question it, but effective training encourages students to appraise critically their theoretical base and recognize its strengths and limitations. We see this as a necessary and integral part of the process through which students learn to assimilate the model in such a way as to make it a genuine part of themselves – their own way of thinking and working. Assimilation involves discrimination between those aspects of the theory that are consistent with the student's subjective values and attitudes and those that in some way do not seem to fit. Any informed discrimination must be grounded in a thorough understanding of the model and takes into account the views of eminent theorists, practitioners and researchers.

In their study of the core model theory, students should be exposed to the findings of process and outcome research studies relevant to any aspect of the core model or its application. However, any piece of research must itself be subject to scrutiny. The basic assumptions and methodology, especially of some of the early research into the efficacy of particular approaches to counselling, may be flawed or the findings may have since been questioned or contradicted by more recent research. Some students may need help to understand academic research studies and to evaluate their findings and conclusions.

Perhaps on all courses, but especially those based on models developed by charismatic figures, it is all too easy for students to idealize the person and approach. There is after all a certain security in feeling you know the 'right way' and of being able to hold on to a set of beliefs, assumptions and methods of working. This heightens the risk that clients are made to fit the model or that students see in their clients what their model implies they should see. In order to develop a realistic and balanced view of their approach, students should become familiar with the criticisms and alternative perspectives on the core model published by established writers and practitioners. Criticism of the core model approach or any of the key concepts, together with any published rebuttals by advocates of the approach or indeed by the course trainers themselves, can contribute lively debate to the teaching and learning of the core model theory. It may be hard for trainers who may have invested many years of study and who work within the particular theoretical frame to encourage scrutiny, albeit informed scrutiny, of that approach. Nevertheless, as Dryden and Feltham (1992, p. 1) point out, counsellors themselves are engaged with their clients in a search for truth and clarity and it would therefore be illogical to resist or fear examination of any aspect of professional practice; this must surely include the core theoretical model.

The argument that students need both to examine critically and acquire an in-depth working knowledge of the core model, may present a potential dilemma with possible implications for selection. At the end of the course students will be assessed on their understanding of the core model and their skills in applying it to their counselling practice. It is possible that some students may discover that they are not able to assimilate the core model to a degree to which it adequately informs their practice. Such students may have an unsatisfactory training experience that will jeopardize their chances of completing the course. Hopefully, this will be a rare occurrence if course publicity makes explicit the nature of the core model and adequate admission and induction procedures enable students to make an informed application in the first place (see Chapter 5).

## ALTERNATIVE MODELS

Learning to compare and contrast one area of study with another is a familiar exercise for students of many subjects. It is a way of getting to grips with a particular topic and learning about concepts and ideas in a wider context. In counsellor training the study of approaches to counselling other than the core model provides external criteria for students to evaluate the strengths and limitations of the model. Students are not required to develop a 'working knowledge' of what we refer to as alternative models, but rather acquire a cognitive understanding of the function and dynamics of related theories of human behaviour and their basic assumptions, key concepts and methods that will enable comparison with the core training model. It is important for students to recognize that their core model is only one way of working and not *the* truth.

Most courses introduce the alternative models component in the second year of training. The logic of this curriculum sequence is that students should first be able to develop an adequate understanding of the core model and feel sufficiently confident and secure in starting work with clients on the basis of their core model, before being asked to examine alternative approaches.

In thinking about the objectives and rationale for the content and structure of the alternative models component, trainers need to consider such questions as: How many alternative models should be introduced? Should they be similar to the core model, perhaps within the same broad tradition as the core model, or should they be from a very different, contrasting theoretical orientation? Are specific models or broad approaches to be studied? For example, a decision might be whether to study Rational Emotive Behaviour Therapy and the work of Albert Ellis as a specific approach, or whether to study the common elements and ideas of cognitive-behavioural approaches more generally. What is the purpose of studying alternative models and how is it intended that they relate to the core model? Is the aim to deepen and enrich the understanding of the core model by comparing and contrasting with other models or is it intended that students be encouraged to explore ways in which explanatory concepts and therapeutic interventions might be integrated within the student's own personal synthesis of the core model? And who answers these questions: the staff or the students themselves?

The way these issues are resolved will to a large extent be determined by the aim and rationale for the whole course and by the nature of the particular core model on which it is based. However, all too often we suspect that the decision about which alternative models to teach comes down to a matter of expediency and simply reflects the current interest and expertise of the available staff, rather than any carefully considered rationale about how the alternative models relate to the core model. We do not believe that there are any necessarily right or wrong answers to these questions, but that it is important that the course has its own answers and a rationale for such a comparison which is communicated to students.

The time allocated to the alternative models component is one factor that influences the number of models introduced and the possible depth of study. The challenge is to achieve a balance between the inevitable superficial coverage of too many approaches and an in-depth study of only one other model closely related to the core model. For example, it could be argued that a Kleinian core model could be compared with a similar psychodynamic approach, but should, ideally, also be contrasted with a humanistic or cognitive-behavioural model. Some courses include the comparison with similar models or at least aspects of similar models, as part of the core model component. The alternative models component would then cover contrasting models.

Courses with an eclectic or integrative core model may include other models or the study of relevant concepts and therapeutic interventions derived from a variety of other models or approaches as a part of the core model component. This may be regarded as adequate in itself, but an alternative models component might examine any one or more approaches to counselling not included in the core model component. Alternatively, it might more usefully compare and contrast working with an eclectic or integrative model with that of a single theoretical system.

## SOCIAL CONTEXT

The BAC Code of Ethics and Practice for Counsellors (BAC, 1993b) states that 'counsellors will take all reasonable steps to take account of the client's social context'. We use the term social context in a generic sense to include such variables as gender, race, culture, religion, age and the wider economic, political, educational, organizational and institutional systems. During training, students should be given ample opportunity to explore these issues from three perspectives.

The first perspective is the social context of human development and the origin and perpetuation of psychological problems. It is possible to identify two extreme positions. In one theoretical position client problems and the explanations relating to client needs for help are located within the individual. In this position social context issues are seen as largely irrelevant to counselling. The same repertoire of counselling skills and strategies is regarded as equally applicable to all clients and no special knowledge of social context variables and their impact on human development and client problems is seen as necessary. Bernard and Goodyear (1992) describe this 'myth of sameness' as an error in which counsellors are convinced that their skills are generic and can be applied to individuals of whatever background. An opposing theoretical view sees human development and the origin and perpetuation of client problems as a function of the interaction between the individual and the environment. From this theoretical position, counsellors would need to develop a working knowledge and high level of awareness of the nature and potential impact of social context. Proponents of this view would argue that it is necessary for counsellors-in-training to learn how to take social context variables into account during assessment and how to adapt their counselling approach in the light of this assessment. Sue and Sue (1990) provide an example of this theoretical position, although they focus on the single contextual variable of cultural difference in which they subsume other social forces. Students need to understand the dynamics of the 'social construction of reality' (see Chapter 11) and how it manifests itself on the therapeutic process.

The second perspective on social context relates to the counselling relationship and the social similarities and differences between the counsellor and client. Bernard and Goodyear (1992) suggest that a good place to start is for counsellors-in-training to explore their own social and ethnic differences as a backdrop to exploring the social and cultural context of others. They argue that understanding our own world view and that of others is the key to multicultural effectiveness. Bernard and Goodyear (1992, p. 206) present Christensen's model of the stages in the development of cross-cultural awareness, which we see as equally applicable to wider social context issues. The five-stage model starts from a position of unawareness of the influence and meaning for individuals or groups of social differences. It then moves through 'beginning awareness' accompanied by uneasiness and a beginning sense of cognitive dissonance, through 'conscious awareness' of the sometimes conflicting preoccupation with social differences and their possible meaning in a historical and present-day context. The fourth stage is characterized by a commitment to understanding and celebrating differences, through to the final stage which moves beyond the limitations of societal dictates regarding what is appropriate and acceptable to appropriate, effortless and spontaneous responses to others. It may be all too easy for students to assume that they are already working within the final developmental stage.

The third perspective is on the social context of counselling itself. Counselling is largely a product of the majority culture. It reflects the values, beliefs, attitudes and language of Western white middle-class society. Here students will be concerned with the analysis of political questions implicit in the activity of counselling. Woolfe (1983) suggests that social control is one of the main social context issues and that the question that needs to be asked is whether counselling is part of the solution for clients or whether in fact it is part of the problem, in as much as it is an agent of social control.

The social context theory element also needs to include some analysis of the dynamics and impact of the various institutional or organizational settings, such as schools, colleges, health or social work. This will be a key issue for courses training counsellors to work in specific fields, for example as student counsellors.

What we argue here is that counsellors-in-training need to examine the implications and meaning of the cultural, social and systemic context of counselling both for themselves and their clients. We are not suggesting that training courses should encourage students to adopt a particular position on social context, but rather that they critically examine social context issues and how these relate to the core training model.

In a useful discussion of social context, Bimrose (1993) identifies various ways of defining social context and the related theoretical perspectives and implications for counselling. She is critical that training courses seem to pay so little attention to social context and suggests that it has remained the invisible issue in relation to counselling theory, training and practice over the past few decades.

## COUNSELLING APPLICATIONS

There is an accumulative wisdom in the growing literature on common client problems and the issues and approaches to counselling with particular client populations. Courses may choose to offer training on the application of the core model to selected presenting problems: examples may include bereavement, anxiety, stress, sexual abuse, crisis and trauma, alcohol and drug misuse, career decision-making, life transitions and other issues, such as therapeutic stuckness or resistance, dependent clients, overly talkative clients or clients who are reluctant or find it difficult to talk. Courses may choose to include workshops on counselling with one or more specific client populations: men, women, children, adolescents, couples, particular ethnic groups. Students need to be aware of the unique concerns of specific client populations, while at the same time recognize the sometimes greater individual differences within them.

The counselling applications component of training may involve presenting the work and views of key theorists on the nature, aetiology and recommended treatment or ways of dealing with specific problems or client populations. Students need to be able to evaluate critically the impact on the core model of any alternative views and approaches. They need to be able to identify the strengths and any apparent conceptual and practical limitations of knowledge about specific problems or populations and be aware of the temptation and risks of using that knowledge predictively.

The topics and areas included in the counselling applications component may be negotiated with the student group so that it can take into account the interests and the nature and range of client work undertaken by the majority of the course group. Only the larger courses may be able to offer an option programme with viable student numbers in each group. What inevitably happens is that this area of the course is often a compromise between the expertise of available staff and student needs and interests. Counselling applications provides an ideal opportunity, finances permitting, to involve people outside the course who currently work with specific presenting problems or client populations. However, it is important that the course helps students to reconcile the core model with any alternative ways of working.

The counselling applications element of training may be organized as a discrete component or taught within other areas of the course, such as the core model, alternative models or contextual psychology component.

## PROFESSIONAL AND CLINICAL PRACTICE

This final aspect of theory is typically subsumed within the core model theory, but may equally well be presented in its own right as an important and substantive component.

The central topic is the relevant code of ethics. On BAC-recognized courses students are required to be formally and explicitly introduced to the BAC Code of Ethics and Practice for Counsellors *before* starting work with clients. They should be given ample opportunity during the course to study and discuss all aspects of the code and to become familiar with its implications for practice and how it relates to their own values and attitudes (BAC, 1990, p. 7). Course staff who provide clinical supervision and those outside the course organization who supervise students on the course need to have a thorough working knowledge of the code.

In this way, students' attention can be drawn to any relevant section of the code and any issues emerging from the students' practice may be discussed and resolved during supervision.

All basic counsellor training will involve clinical supervision and students may find it interesting and helpful to study some of the key concepts and theory of supervision as part of the professional practice component.

Counsellors-in-training should have the opportunity to discuss the fact that counselling is only one of the ways of responding to the needs of clients within the mental health field. Students need to develop an understanding of the work of other professionals and have the opportunity for meeting with at least some of them. While this is another obvious area for outside speakers, many courses effectively utilize the resources of the student group. The typical profile of almost any cohort of counselling students will include people with basic professional training and current experience of working in other areas of mental health. Perhaps students themselves remain an underused resource and here is the ideal opportunity for some kind of learning exchange in which students share with each other their knowledge and experience of working in different areas of mental health.

Another aspect of theory that needs to be covered in some part of a counsellor training is what we describe as clinical practice issues: stages of the therapeutic process, beginning and ending work with clients, principles and practice of referral, writing case notes, record-keeping, contracting, client assessment and history-taking, use of diagnostic classification systems, audiotape recording, homework or client assignments, application of psychometric tests and the evaluation of process and outcomes. Some of these issues are common to most forms of counselling, but the choice of others will be determined by the nature of the core model.

## APPROACHES TO TEACHING AND LEARNING

So far we have looked at the main theory elements of counsellor training. We now turn to the ways and means of facilitating teaching and learning.

Faced with economic pressure to increase student numbers, courses tend to teach theory in large groups through traditional lecture methods. In many institutions this didactic approach is still seen as the most expedient way of teaching theory, but it is not necessarily the most effective. Currently this is very much an issue in higher education generally and one response has been to improve presentation and communication skills, making greater use of audiovisual aids in the process. This response may not always bring most benefits and as counsellor trainers are fully aware, it can serve to hide the more substantial issue that lectures, however inspiring and well presented, have limited outcomes. Students can easily slip into the role of passive listeners and become bored or acquiescent. Andresen (1990, p. 9) suggests that 'students respond to our teaching styles in the only way they know and that is by doing what they think we want them to do'. Higher education can learn much from counsellor training and the emphasis we tend to place on experiential and more interactive learning and teaching. Even with lectures it is possible to abandon teaching as a monologue and work towards increased dialogue, in which students are more actively engaged. For example, the introduction of five minutes' open discussion (clarification, questions and feedback) soon after the start of a lecture can generate new levels of energy. After about 25 minutes most audiences begin to grow inattentive and tired of listening. A similar idea is the five- to ten-minute buzz group at critical points of the lecture. Here students form pairs with the task of discussing their reactions and the application of the new ideas. An extension to this is the technique of 'snowballing' in which students are first invited to reflect alone on the material presented, then share their ideas, first in pairs, then fours before returning to the whole group or plenary, and pooling conclusions, issues and feedback. Leaving 'any questions' to the end of a formal lecture often results in the proverbial deafening silence.

Students are usually avid collectors of handouts, pleased to receive them and often critical if none are given out, yet frequently they never refer back to them. An alternative is for trainers to produce skeleton or incomplete handouts identifying key concepts or the main points of the lecture. This forces students away from docile note-taking, encouraging them to pay attention to the meaning of what is being presented and enabling them to add their own detailed notes in the spaces on the handout. Some trainers preclude extensive note-taking by giving students the precise text and chapter where everything they need to know can be found and on other occasions deliberately highlight crucial points by suggesting that students need to 'write this down'. At the end of theory sessions, time can be given for students to swap notes to check all the main points, correcting or adding to their own. This can be a productive buzz group activity. Extensive use of detailed OHP transparencies can be frustrating for students trying to get it all down on paper and missing the trainer's commentary in doing so. It can be helpful to photocopy transparencies and reduce the size so that four fit onto one side of A4 paper. This makes a convenient handout.

Brainstorming is a technique which can involve everybody in small groups and can help overcome the fear of ridicule when students are asked to give their ideas and opinions. Brainstorming invites students to express their ideas freely, however simple or apparently outrageous.

At the beginning of a session, the result of a brainstorm can give the trainer a sense of what students already know about the subject, or used later it can generate creative ideas about the topic being studied.

Demonstrations are an important part of most theory sessions. They can be defined as anything the tutor does during the session that can be described as showing students as distinct from telling them. Demonstrations may involve audiovisual aids, modelling a particular skill, procedure or performance, presenting an actual or simulated situation that poses a specific question for students to ponder or illustrates the application of a particular concept.

Gibbs and Habeshaw (1984) have produced a useful publication, *Interesting Things to Do in Your Lectures*. It contains many ideas easily adapted to counsellor training and is especially useful when teaching theory in large groups.

Counsellor trainers are familiar with other methods of organizing teaching and learning: seminars, workshops with short lecturettes followed by structured exercises, small group discussions and feedback, case discussion groups, student-led groups and individual or small group presentations by students. One of the most successful ways of learning theory is to set up small study groups of four/five students who work together to prepare a presentation to the course group.

Theory informs all aspects of counselling practice, but theory is seldom taught effectively if it is only regarded as a separate activity from other forms of learning. Students will raise theoretical questions that emerge from their own practice during supervision, skills training laboratories and large group meetings, even though these activities are ostensibly about other things. Staff and indeed other students can respond by reference to appropriate theory and recommend further reading. Mearns (1993, p. 29) points out that 'it is astounding how often people equate the learning of theory with boredom in lectures'. A similar notion is that 'if we aren't taking notes we can't be learning'! We are not, of course, advocating that essential theory should only be structured around questions students raise at various times in the course, but simply that there are many opportunities for grounding theory in practice that serve to complement more formal presentations.

Theory is one of the major elements of counsellor training, yet it has hitherto often been the poor relation of skills training on courses developed outside universities and other educational institutions. The reverse has tended to be true on those courses established in higher education settings, where all too frequently, the emphasis has been on academic work to the almost total exclusion of skills training. Skill training is an essential element of counsellor training and we will look at its related issues in the next chapter.

# SEVEN
# Skills training

In this chapter, we will focus on the place that skills training has in professional counsellor training. More particularly, we will discuss (a) the nature of these skills and the role that they have in the practice of counselling; (b) the relationship between counselling skills and the core theoretical model; (c) when counselling skills training should take place on professional counsellor training courses; (d) who should teach counselling skills; and (e) how such training is generally done.

## THE NATURE OF COUNSELLING SKILLS

What exactly are counselling skills? Unfortunately, there is no simple answer to this question and, furthermore, there is no consensus view on this issue within the fields of counselling and counsellor training. Let us consider these different views.

Some people consider a counselling skill to be a discrete unit of behaviour (verbal, non-verbal and para-verbal). Taking this view, we may think of discrete responses such as paraphrasing, reflecting feelings and the like as counselling skills and even smaller units of behaviour (e.g. minimal encouragers to talk, mm-mmh's, head nods) as micro-skills.

Other people think of skills as comprising larger units or sequences made up of smaller units. Taking this view, we may think of making interpretations and confrontation as 'larger unit' skills.

A further view considers the skilful application of theoretical concepts as skills. For example, such people would talk of the communication of empathy or dealing with transference as skills. However, these are really theoretical concepts which can be skilfully or non-skilfully applied in practice.

A final view regards the skilful execution of therapeutic tasks as skills. For example, setting an agenda is regarded as an important therapeutic task in Cognitive-Behavioural counselling and might be regarded as a skill within that specialism, though, once again, it is properly classified as a task that can again be executed skilfully or non-skilfully.

While most theorists think of counselling skills as observable units of behaviour of variable complexity, others consider counselling skills to include unobservable phenomena. Such people would talk of the skills of awareness and clinical decision-making, both of which comprise a set of unobservable internal events. Our own view is to regard skills as involving only observable units of behaviour, while fully recognizing the importance of such internal counsellor activity as awareness and clinical decision-making which are best considered as abilities of reflective practitioners rather than as skills.

Whichever view trainers take of counselling skills, it is important that they realize that the purpose of counselling skills training is to help trainees demonstrate competence in the generic and approach-specific skills which are emphasized by the core theoretical model, not only with trainee 'clients' but with real clients. To this end, trainers need to develop relevant ways of assessing trainee competence in the use of counselling skills for use in both the counselling practicum and actual counselling settings (see Chapter 12 and the volume by Wheeler (in preparation) in this series on assessment in counsellor training).

## COUNSELLING SKILLS AND THE CORE THEORETICAL MODEL

Certain counselling skills, such as active listening, encouraging clients to talk and the communication of empathy, are probably regarded as important skills by most, if not all, counselling approaches. As such, they can best be seen as generic counselling skills. Where the influence of the core theoretical model on counselling skills becomes most apparent is when we consider what counsellor trainers may regard as more advanced skills. These are the skills that are closely associated with the core theoretical model. As such, we refer to them here as approach-specific skills. Examples of approach-specific skills might be the skill of disputing irrational beliefs in Rational Emotive Behaviour Therapy, the skill of conducting a two-chair dialogue in Gestalt Therapy and the skill of facilitiating the client's focusing in Person-Centred Therapy.

If we use Beitman's (1987) framework introduced in Chapter 3, we might say that while the more generic counselling skills are used throughout counselling, they are particularly predominant in the engagement stage and the early part of the pattern-search stage. The approach-specific skills, on the other hand, come more to the fore in the latter part of the pattern-search stage and throughout the pattern-change stage.

## WHEN SHOULD SKILLS TRAINING TAKE PLACE?

Counselling skills training should be initiated on professional counselling courses as soon as possible. Since the major objective of professional counsellor training is to produce competent counsellors, the main emphasis of the early part of a professional counselling course is on preparing trainees to see clients as quickly as possible. Counselling skills training plays a crucial role in this preparation stage. However, it is important that students comprehend the rationale and function of such skills and understand their place in the counselling approach that informs the course. This means that staff need to present students with an overview of the core theoretical model. Without this students will be taught counselling skills in a theoretical vacuum and may not fully understand the rationale for learning such skills.

Counselling skills training may continue throughout the entire course or at least for a major part of it. This is especially likely to be the case when the counselling approach that informs the course is one that is heavily skills-based such as the 'skilled helper' model of Gerard Egan (1994). In such cases the teaching of counselling skills usually follows the same order as that in which the skills tend to be used with clients, with the generic skills – which are heavily used in the engagement stage and the early stage of pattern-search – being covered first and the approach-specific skills – which are employed more in the later phase of pattern-search and throughout the pattern-change stage – being covered later.

This last point is important. On professional counsellor training courses there is an essential tension between the ideal of having trainees thoroughly prepared before the start of client work and the pragmatic position which holds that since training time is limited and theory and skills practice often only begins to make sense in relation to actual client work, trainees should start seeing clients as soon as possible. This need to move into client work means that staff have to be clear with one another and with students concerning the skills at which trainees need to demonstrate competence before seeing clients and those skills which can be learned later, during client work.

So far we have dealt with the situation where counselling skills training is a deliberately undertaken activity with its own regular, timetabled slot on the curriculum. However, we do wish to make the point that informal skills training may permeate the course and occur, albeit briefly, at other times during the course. For example, in group supervision, a supervisor might model a skilful way of responding to a client, then ask the supervisee to practise this new response in a role-play with a fellow supervisee and provide feedback on the performance. Such informal skills training may take place at any time during the course, although in our view, course staff and supervisors need to have a detailed understanding of where trainees are in their development before embarking upon what might be called 'incidental, informal skills training'. Otherwise there is a danger that they may try to teach skills that are too advanced for the trainee's current stage of development as a counsellor.

## WHO SHOULD TEACH COUNSELLING SKILLS?

Counselling skills training should be taught by senior trainers who are themselves highly skilled and effective practitioners. As such, and reiterating the point that we underscored in Chapter 4, counselling skills trainers should maintain an ongoing counselling caseload. In addition, counselling skills trainers should be prepared to play audiotaped excerpts from their own counselling work to demonstrate these skills in action. However, not all counsellor trainers make good counselling skills trainers, so let us outline some of the tasks of a skills trainer to illustrate the types of activities at which he or she has to be competent.

One of the tasks of the counselling skills trainer is to be a competent modeller of the generic and approach-specific counselling skills which comprise the skills training curriculum. Here, the trainer has to be comfortable demonstrating these skills in front of the trainee cohort. She has to make judicious and sensitive selections concerning the trainees who will play 'clients' in these demonstrations, choosing trainees who are not overly invested in making her look good or look bad in front of the training group, or trainees who are currently working through particular emotional problems.

It used to be the case that trainers could work with small trainee groups in the skills training part of the course. Even a skills trainer/ trainee ratio of one to four was not uncommon twenty years ago. Nowadays, this would be considered a luxury and ratios of one skills trainer to ten trainees are more common. Our view is that a 1:12 staff–student ratio should be the maximum for skills training. If all trainees are to be given an opportunity each week to practise and receive trainer feedback on the target skill, this necessitates the trainer moving from trainee dyad to dyad (or triad to triad if a trainee observer is used) to ensure that this is done. These days, therefore, the effective skills trainer has to be comfortable and adept at observing brief segments of trainee skills practice, formulating helpful feedback in a short period of time and offering this in a constructive way. Trainers have to be able to think quickly on their feet (literally sometimes) as they move from group to group.

A recent development is the greater use being made of trainee trainers in the skills training component of the course. As long as this is done under the supervision of a senior trainer, this can be constructive for both the trainee and the counsellor-in-training. However, since the senior trainer cannot be in two places at once, the trainee trainer will often tape-record the 'counselling' segments that they observe, and also their feedback, for later review and supervision.

## HOW IS COUNSELLING SKILLS TRAINING DONE?

In this section, we will outline in depth one approach to counselling skills training to illustrate how skills training can be tackled. For another approach to skills training (broadly defined) which is more consistent with psychodynamic counselling see Jacobs (1991).

It is important to distinguish between two basic elements of effective counsellor communication: an ability to *discriminate* well and the ability to make helpful *responses*. By our definition, the first is best viewed as an internal activity of reflective practitioners while the second can be properly regarded as a skill. However, both form a part of counselling skills training.

## Discrimination and response training

Since an ability to make accurate discriminations precedes skilful responding to what clients have to say, discrimination training with reference to a particular counselling skill is frequently done first in skills training. The focus of discrimination training is on helping trainees to discriminate between accurate and inaccurate formulations of what clients communicate and between helpful and unhelpful responses to these communications with reference to the target skill. Exercises designed to increase trainees' ability to discriminate include the presentation of client communications on audio, video or in the form of written statements. Then, trainees are provided with a number of options which detail (a) accurate and inaccurate representations of the client's experience and, thereafter, (b) helpful and unhelpful responses to that experience with reference to a particular skill. Trainees are then asked to select an option that best represents the client's experience and the most helpful response. After this, trainees are asked to give reasons for their choices and trainers give relevant feedback, helping trainees to understand reasons for their correct and incorrect selections.

When trainees are able to make accurate discriminations and responses with reference to a particular skill, the emphasis moves on to encourage using the skill to a high degree of competence.

## The process of skills training

Another way of looking at counselling skills training is to view it as a *process*. This is what Ford (1979) did in an excellent review of research into counselling skills training. He conceptualized counselling skills training as involving *instruction*, *modelling practice* and *feedback*. In discussing this process we will take the situation where one skill is taught at a time.

INSTRUCTION

Instruction is used throughout the counselling skills process, but is particularly salient at the outset in both a general sense and a specific sense. In the general sense, at the beginning of a skills training group the tutor will explain verbally (and with reference to handouts and relevant texts) the overall model of skills training that is to be employed during this component of the course. This model may be one already in existence, an amalgam of what is available or one devised by the tutor. Whichever approach is used it is important that trainees are given an overall picture of the model as well as its purpose and have an opportunity to discuss it before specific skills are introduced. Some courses will choose to do this in the theory part of the course as part of the teaching of the core theoretical model. In this way they illustrate the interaction between theory and skills training.

When specific skills are introduced, instruction to explain the skill and give guidance on its purpose and limits is helpful before the trainer models the particular skill.

MODELLING

After a skill has been introduced and explained, many trainers (but not all) demonstrate or present in some way a good model of the skill to be learned. Ford (1979) notes that there are three issues that need to be considered when modelling is carried out: the model; the message; and the medium.

*The model.* It is likely that a *coping* model (i.e. one that is good enough, but not perfect) is more helpful than one which portrays a perfectly skilful performance (i.e a mastery model) in encouraging trainees to practise the skill with confidence. A *mastery* model can lead trainees to feel hopeless about learning the skill since they believe that they will never achieve such flawless performance, while a coping model is more credible to trainees and tends to instil hope. It is for this reason that flawless live performance by trainers and perfectly executed examples of the skill by master practitioners on videotape have their limitations as effective models, at least until trainees have developed competence in the target skill.

*The message.* With respect to the message, it is important, as noted above, that demonstration of effective and ineffective examples of the skill be highlighted so that trainees can learn to discriminate accurately before being expected to execute the skill effectively. If effective audio or video models are presented, relevant cues (for example, audible tones, captions and 'voice over' commentaries) need to be employed if trainees are to be helped to recognize the skill when it is embedded in counselling interactions.

*The medium.* Models can be presented through a variety of media: they can be performed live, demonstrated on videotape, heard on audiotape, displayed through photographs or presented in written, transcript form. Obviously, the target skill will determine to a large extent the medium used. For example, non-verbal skills require a visual medium, e.g. live modelling, videotape demonstration or photographs. Consequently, courses need to be well resourced if they are to use different media to model different skills. (See Chapter 4 for a full discussion of the resources needed to run a professional counselling training course.)

We mentioned earlier that not all trainers use modelling at this stage of the counselling skills training process. Some trainers fear that exposure to models at this point might lead trainees to imitate the model rather than integrate the skill into their natural style of responding. Thus, such tutors proceed directly from instruction to practice and use modelling at a later stage of the skills training process, when trainees have established their own counselling style. While we understand this concern, we also recognize that imitation is more likely to be a problem when trainees are frequently exposed to high status models such as their tutors, the founders of the counselling approach which informs the course or leading figures in that approach. However, if the target skills are modelled by ordinary practitioners of the approach the 'imitation problem' is minimized.

PRACTICE

When trainees are given an opportunity to practise the skill under consideration (referred to here as the target skill), there are different ways in which this can be done. Perhaps the most frequently used approach is 'peer counselling', in which one trainee counsels a fellow trainee for a specified period of time. The question then arises as to whether the 'client' discusses a real concern or adopts the role of a client and invents a problem.

The main advantage of the 'real problem' situation is that the 'client' can refer to his own feelings during the counselling session and can give reliable feedback to the 'counsellor' concerning the impact of the target skill. Also the 'client' can be successfully helped to explore a significant personal issue by the peer 'counsellor', showing both of them that trainees can be helpful in the counselling role. Finally, if the 'client' discusses a personal concern in the practice stage of counselling skills training, this emphasizes the interactive nature of professional counsellor training.

The main disadvantage of the trainee 'clients' choosing to talk about personal issues in skills training practice is that they may go further in their exploration than they anticipated and become distressed as a result. In such cases, the amount and quality of support present on the course is a crucial factor in determining the impact of this situation on the distressed trainee. In many respects, trainers are responsible for creating a 'holding' environment for their trainees. An obvious, but sometimes neglected maxim here is: 'Put the welfare of the trainee before skills practice' if the two conflict. This is why it is so important that trainees have a suitable context in which to explore their concerns, be this in personal therapy or in a personal development group. If skills training is the only forum which trainees have to explore themselves, the boundaries between skills training and personal development become too blurred, with unfortunate consequences. In such cases, trainees will neither have sufficient time for learning skills, nor adequate opportunity to explore their personal concerns at length and in depth. This is one of the reasons why a course will not be recognized by the BAC if it claims that skills training is the major forum that trainees have for personal development.

Another drawback to having trainees use personal material when in the 'client' role in skills training is that the material they choose to discuss may not be suitable for the practice of the target skill by the 'counsellor'. Thus, if the target skill is 'challenging', the 'client' may not be ready to be challenged on his problem. Thus, the trainee 'client' needs to consult with the trainer concerning the selection of a relevant personal issue, if the 'counsellor' is to gain useful practice in the target skill and if 'clients' are to gain benefit from discussing their personal concerns.

The main disadvantage of a trainee *role-playing* a client in skills practice is that 'clients' can either abandon the role in an attempt to be a 'good' client for their colleague or may stick rigidly to the role, negating any helpful shift in experience as a result of counselling. It is a skill in itself to portray accurately a role with the right degree of flexibility. Trainees playing a client 'role', therefore, need a good deal of help to do this. First, the role needs to be appropriate to the skill that is being taught. Second, the instructions given to the 'client' about the role need to be full enough for the trainee to play it adequately. This itself is an exercise in empathy as the trainee struggles to get inside the frame of reference of the 'client'. Because of the complexity involved in adhering to a client role in a flexible manner, some courses on occasion use actors to play the role of clients, although the expense of doing so precludes this being a regular part of skills training. Actors are particularly useful when portrayal of profound problems is required. For example, an actor can research and fully portray a psychotic client in a thoroughly convincing fashion, yet he or she can be trusted to retain a firm hold of their own reality. When using actors it is important to give them advance warning that the work is unscripted and that they will be expected not to stick rigidly to their initial position but to roll with the counsellor's responses.

The main advantage of the use of role-playing in skills training practice is that it safeguards the welfare of trainees, while giving them the opportunity to practise skills in response to 'client' material (as long as the client role approximates to the problems of real clients). An additional advantage of role-playing is that if trainees become proficient at it, they can play the role of their own clients and learn more about them in the process, often with great immediacy.

Other approaches to skills practice involve trainees responding to brief written, audiotaped or videotaped 'client' vignettes. Genuine clients should not be involved in counselling skills training.

FEEDBACK

Trainees will best learn and refine their counselling skills if they are given feedback. If this is to take place then, of course, the person giving the feedback needs to observe the trainee performance directly. One way is through live observation. Here feedback can be given at the end of an observed sequence or even during it, either through interruption or by means of 'bug in the ear' devices (where the trainer communicates privately via a microphone to the trainee who is wearing an earphone). How and when feedback is given in this respect can vary according to the trainee's preference.

Feedback can be also be given in response to audiotaped or videotaped counselling sessions, video being particularly suitable when the target counselling skills are non-verbal. However, trainees will need to become comfortable using these media before benefiting fully from such feedback.

Ford (1979) has noted that there are four issues concerning feedback: the message; feedback valence; the medium; and the source.

*The feedback message.* With respect to the message, feedback may be a simple right or wrong response or it may include information which (a) encourages better discrimination; (b) provides greater explanation than had been given hitherto; and (c) involves the use of modelling. The main research finding concerning the message component of feedback is that performance-specific feedback is more effective than non-specific feedback in aiding the acquisition of the target skill (Ford, 1979).

*The valence of feedback.* The valence of feedback can be positive or negative or provide neutral descriptions of behaviour. Our experience is that judiciously given positive feedback with specific information and instructions concerning future performance is the type of feedback found most useful by trainees, although this issue needs to be researched. Consistently negative feedback is destructive and demoralizing, consistently positive feedback has a Pollyanna-ish quality to it which leads trainees to doubt the sincerity of the feedback source, while consistently neutral (or informational) feedback leaves trainees wondering about how well or poorly they are using counselling skills.

*The medium of feedback.* Feedback is usually given verbally, although written feedback is also given by trainers in interim or final assessments of trainee performance in skills training groups. The use of numerical feedback is also relevant if the trainer is using scales (such as Carkhuff's (1969) five-point scales of counsellor facilitative functioning) to indicate a range of skill levels.

*The source of feedback.* The source of feedback can be the trainer, the trainee 'client', an observer (if counselling triads are employed) or the trainee 'counsellor' giving feedback to herself or himself. All four are best used in rotation, unless this becomes confusing for the trainee. If trainer feedback alone is preferred, this communicates to trainees that their views are unimportant, while if only trainees' feedback is elicited the trainer's expertise is not utilized. Here, as elsewhere in professional counsellor training, a healthy balance should be sought. When trainee feedback is used, it is helpful if trainees are first given guidelines concerning how to give effective feedback. Otherwise, peer feedback may be useless at best or damaging at worst.

Interpersonal Process Recall (IPR) methods (Kagan, 1984) can be very helpful during later stages of counselling skills training in teasing out the covert and difficult-to-identify elements of trainee experience in the role of both 'counsellor' and 'client' during skills training. Using an adapted form of IPR, the trainer (or someone else) replays the tape (video or audio) of the counselling session, encouraging the 'counsellor' and/or 'client' to stop the tape whenever they want to discuss an important point related to the target skill and which has been stimulated by listening to or watching the tape. This method allows the 'counsellor' and 'client' to reflect not only on the observable skill but on their thoughts and feelings before, during and after the event, thus helping the participants to analyse the counsellor's processing as well as his or her behaviour. These experiential elements often shed light on the skills practice session, which might otherwise be neglected if the emphasis in skills training is exclusively on observable skills.

While IPR should not itself be used exclusively in skills training since it was not designed to facilitate skill acquisition (Baker *et al.*, 1990; Kagan and Kagan, 1990), it can be usefully employed as an adjunct in skills training to tease out relevant covert experiences which need to be processed along with the focus on observable skills. Arguably, the IPR method is the one which most directly practises the skills of being a 'reflective practitioner'.

## The integration of skills

So far we have considered the situation where skills are introduced one at a time. However, later in skills training, trainees need help in integrating these skills so that they can make use of them as required with their clients. The skills training sessions may now focus on audio/video tapes of whole counselling sessions, helping trainees to analyse the skills employed and how those skills were interwoven into a smooth performance reflective of the individual style of the counsellor.

Supervision is another forum where counsellors-in-training can explore their integration of skills. At a simple level, the supervisor (who needs up-to-date knowledge of the skills which trainees have covered) can suggest the use of skills as part of their supervisory feedback. At a more advanced level, the audiotapes which trainees make of their current real counselling work can be analysed to explore the integration of skills and developing style of the counsellor-in-training.

The approach to skills training illustrated by this chapter follows the inherently logical structure of considering skills individually at first before seeking to integrate these skills later in training. However, it should be noted that not all core theoretical models would follow that same sequence so rigidly. For example, there is a preference in Person-Centred training to place greater emphasis on integration fr the outset and seeing the skills training task as one of helping trainee to become aware of where they stand on numerous ski' not dictating the *order* in which they challenge their own dev of these skills.

Having considered the role of skills training in professional counsellor training courses, we will change tack and look at the issue of fostering trainee self-development.

# EIGHT
# Self-development

In this chapter we shall discuss the relevance of self-development in counselling training and the various ways in which courses endeavour to facilitate that development through personal therapy, personal development groups and the keeping of personal journals. We hold the view that counsellors-in-training benefit from a variety of personal development activities, tailored to meet the unique needs of the individual.

It might be argued that since every dimension of self may, at one time or another, be relevant to the work with clients then *any* self-development work is relevant to counselling training. However, the argument does not follow that the trainee may simply focus on any aspects of self-development by whatever means and thereby meet the self-development requirement of training. This is sometimes the approach taken by individuals unsupported and unstimulated by a good training context – they tend to restrict their self-development to the most attractive areas without regard to or even awareness of broader or deeper personal development needs.

The personal development needs of trainees go beyond personal preferences. Certainly, the trainee will be able to identify some needs with respect to personal development but other people may have an important contribution to make in helping the trainee to become aware of what might otherwise be 'blind spots'. For example, the supervisor, because of his or her closeness to the trainee's work, may be able to identify areas of personal development need. In this regard the supervisor is usually able to offer more if the supervision is based on the analysis of audiotaped work. Take, for example, the challenge: 'Your voice seems to be more strident and cold when you are working with men – I wonder if that's true and if so where it comes from?'

Fellow trainees and tutors have an important role with respect to helping the student to identify areas of self-development need through review of counselling tapes, but also in skills practice settings and in the way the trainee relates with others in the various group work contexts offered by the course. This is one of the reasons why counselling training emphasizes the importance of maintaining the student cohort throughout training, so that challenges develop in a climate of trust and support. The following challenge from a fellow student was difficult for the trainee to accept initially, but later opened up a whole area of personal development need which had not emerged in two years of previous therapy: 'You seem very dismissive of others when their view is not exactly the same as your own. You huff and puff and often turn away and sneer. It seems to affect you an awful lot.'

Hence, the self-development needs of the trainee are broader than those which he or she might immediately identify. The list below details just some of the self-development goals which a counselling training course might hold. This list is taken from a BAC-recognized course whose core theoretical model is Person-Centred. The language used by courses of other traditions would be different but many of the areas depicted would likely be similar.

## SELF-DEVELOPMENT AIMS

As a result of their experience of the training, participants will be able to exhibit awareness, knowledge and attributes within each of the following categories:

SELF-STRUCTURE

(i)    awareness of introjected beliefs about self and how these influence the self-concept and behaviour;

(ii)   awareness of personal processes of dissonance reduction and how these are involved in the social construction of reality;

(iii)  understanding how social and personality dynamics have influenced the development of self;

(iv)   understanding the conditions of worth which operated in one's own early development and how these continue to influence the self-concept, personal development and work with clients;

(v)    identification of the stages of movement through personal transitional experiences;

(vi)   development of a sufficiently strong sense of personal identity to resist being drawn into the client's pathology;

(vii)  the achievement of 'self-acceptance', or significant movement in that direction.

## SELF IN RELATION TO OTHERS

(i)   awareness of introjected beliefs about others and how these influence person perception and behaviour;

(ii)  awareness of enduring patterns in one's own interpersonal behaviour and the needs and fears upon which these patterns are based;

(iii) awareness of the assumptions, introjections, needs and fears upon which personal prejudices are based;

(iv)  reduction or control of the influences of personal prejudices;

(v)   awareness of the way in which own sexuality is expressed within personal and professional relationships;

(vi)  understanding of *personal* (as distinct from psychological) theories of human behaviour.

(vii) challenging the dimensions of self which inhibit the achievement of mutuality in therapeutic relationships;

## SELF IN RELATION TO CLIENTS

(i)   awareness of the ways in which personal prejudices influence judgement and behaviour in the counselling setting;

(ii)  awareness of 'blocks' inhibiting personal development with respect to expression of the 'therapeutic conditions' of empathy, unconditional positive regard and congruence;

(iii) understanding of the dynamics of self which create vulnerability to clinical 'over-involvement';

(iv)  understanding of the dynamics of self which create vulnerability to clinical 'under-involvement';

(v)   awareness of the behaviour which encourages projections from clients and questioning the motivation underpinning those behaviours.

## SELF AS A LEARNER

(i)   the ability to develop personal learning goals;

(ii)  a disposition to examine critically and systematically personal understandings, attitudes and skills;

(iii) a confidence to tolerate and learn from the uncertainty which may stem from having assumptions and attitudes challenged;

(iv)  a disposition of openness to experience as it relates to the self, and an acceptance of responsibility for one's own behaviour and learning;

(v)   the ability to use consultation as a part of the process of self-assessment;

(vi)  the capacity to self-appraise openly and accurately.

As a result of training each course member will portray a different pattern of needs with respect to these personal development goals, therefore the course must create learning structures which are highly individualized and indeed which offer a variety of opportunities to face the issues involved in each goal. (Paraphrased from Mearns, 1993b.)

Individual difference requires us to recognize that every trainee would be different in his or her profile of self-development needs. In any of the sample self-development goals listed above some students might require considerable development while others might have attained sufficiency in the area before even embarking upon the training. For this reason it is essential to take an individualized learning approach to personal development, creating learning situations which do not address specific personal development needs, but allow the trainee to explore those which are relevant to himself or herself. Three of the most common of these learning contexts are personal therapy, personal development groups and the keeping of personal journals.

## PERSONAL THERAPY

The BAC courses recognition booklet includes the criterion:

> ensure that trainees gain experience of being in the client role
> (beyond that which is created in skills training and role-plays).
> (BAC, 1990, p. 5).

While this criterion requires experience as a client it does not demand prior or on-going personal therapy. This reflects the general approach taken by BAC course recognition in demanding that certain *functions* (such as self-development) be met but not being over-prescriptive on the *structures* which must be used.

Numerous counselling training courses have a requirement for on-going personal therapy during training. That requirement ranges from an expectation that students will have a minimum of 12 hours therapy during the training to others which demand one hour per week, or even more. Even courses which do not have a personal therapy requirement find that a proportion of their students will voluntarily enter therapy during training.

The research literature suggests that there is no clear relationship between personal therapy and counsellor efficacy (Bergin and Garfield, 1994). However, generally speaking, although it is an expensive addition to training, on-going personal therapy provides great personal support and also a context in which students can explore the roots of any personal issues arising during training and work with clients. The focused individual attention offered by personal therapy can reach depths which are not easily attained in other training contexts and may well contribute, albeit indirectly, to clinical effectiveness as a counsellor.

There is danger in presuming that on-going personal therapy is *sufficient* to cover the range of personal development that is required in training. A lot depends on how closely the personal therapy is linked to the training. There is a tendency for courses to demand on-going personal therapy but thereafter to take absolutely no part in what happens in the therapy, believing, quite justifiably, that it is important not to interfere in the therapy relationship. Simply requiring on-going personal therapy in this way can mean that the therapy focuses only on the most pressing needs of the trainee. It may go to great depth in relation to those needs but it may not cover sufficient breadth for counselling training. However, it is possible to conceive of the on-going therapy as 'training therapy' in the sense that issues arising in other training contexts are referred to the therapy for attention. Usually this happens somewhat informally, with the trainee being invited by tutors or supervisor to 'take that to your therapy', but it is possible to instigate more formal structures of referral and of assessment of outcome whereby, for example, the trainee reports back on that personal development issue after exploring it in therapy.

Some theoretical models (for example, psychodynamic) strongly endorse personal therapy as a part of training. Nevertheless, it is important that training courses do not simply presume that all the personal development needs will be met by making a requirement for individual therapy but that they have ways of linking that therapy into the broad range of personal development needs or have additional or even alternative means of uncovering and working on those needs.

## PERSONAL DEVELOPMENT GROUPS

Just as training therapy will focus on the personal development needs identified as relevant to the counsellor training and practice, the personal development group will have a similar aim rather than function as a free-ranging therapy group focusing on other personal needs unrelated to counselling or training. This boundary between therapy gr      and personal development groups is important. While it would be r a therapy group to devote a lot of time to the member's of her or his difficulties in relation to their partner, th generally speaking, not relevant to the personal devel except insofar as the issue might involve dynamics relevant in the person's on-going training or counsell'

The personal development group is not only a

can be explored: it is also a vibrant context for *identifying* personal development needs. If an atmosphere of trust and spirit of encounter can be developed in the group, the members can help each other to identify needs which might otherwise have been blind spots. Thus, personal development group members may help each other at all stages of negotiating a personal development issue as depicted in the diagram below and in the example which follows.

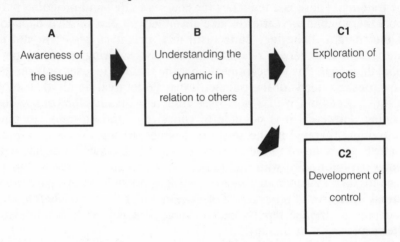

EXAMPLE

Nobody in the personal development group doubted John's attentiveness and caring for clients. Furthermore, he was generally regarded as being more knowledgeable about counselling than anyone else in the group. Yet there was a quality about John which had made it difficult for others to feel really close to him. In a way, it seemed that he was almost too competent. It was only after some months of meeting in the group that one member voiced what others had sensed but not in such a fully-formed fashion. She observed that for a long time she had deferred to him and that that deferring was not so much a response to *what* he said but the *way* he said it and his general demeanour. The way she experienced him was as 'behaving in a very powerful way'. Her clarity helped others to voice their own experiences. One person said that she had felt exactly the same but had presumed that it was her own tendency to feel inferior which was the source of the difficulty. It was difficult for John to hear this because he genuinely felt that he was warm and open to these people and in no way wanted to be experienced as 'powerful'. In a crossover between his personal development group and his supervision group, he began to look at how he behaved in the counselling relationship. Sure enough, when he asked others to listen to audiotapes of his work they confirmed that if they had been the client they might have felt considerably inferior to his rather commanding persona. The supervision group was able to help him to monitor his way of relating to clients through later tapes, and back in the personal development group John explored the disjunction between his outward behaviour and his inner feeling, dipping into the roots in his earlier life (stage C1) and also actively experimenting with different ways of being in relation to others in the group (stage C2).

This example represents a fairly typical use of the personal development group and also the interaction between personal development and supervision. The personal development group is one of many groupings in the training course which, if the right spirit of encounter is established, can help members to become aware of personal development issues (stage A) and understand the interpersonal dynamics relating to those issues (stage B). Thereafter, the group can help the member to explore the roots of the issue (stage C1) as well as developing other ways of being (stage C2). Had John been in on-going training therapy that would also have been a useful place to refer further exploration of the roots. However, it is relevant to note that while individual therapy is a good place for exploring issues already identified, it may not be as powerful as groups for actually identifying the problem. John had spent one and a half years in prior therapy without this issue ever being identified.

There is considerable debate among trainers as to whether personal development groups should be facilitated by core staff members or by staff who are more peripheral to the training and not involved in assessment. The BAC Course Recognition Scheme is not structurally prescriptive on this issue but recognizes that much can be said on both sides.

The argument for using core staff is that, in most core theoretical models, personal development is so central that it cannot be left to the periphery. For example, the Person-Centred trainer may argue that the 'self' of the counsellor is the set of 'tools' by which counselling is achieved. It is so central that the staff would be abrogating responsibility to externalize responsibility for self-development.

The main argument for using external staff concerns the management of boundaries and potentially conflicting roles. It is implicitly tied to the assessment function usually held by core staff. If the assessment role of the core staff results in trainees being reluctant to divulge and explore aspects of self lest they be assessed as incompetent or inadequate, then the personal development functions are in danger of not being met in personal development groups led by a member of the core staff team.

The dilemma about who should run personal development groups thus becomes a symptom of the difficulty which assessment brings to counsellor training. If the assessment process can be opened up in such a way that it is not so exclusively focused on the judgement of core tutors, perhaps broadening it to include self-assessment and peer assessment, then the difficulty may be diluted. Also, the general nature of the relationship developed between core staff and students will make a difference. If that relationship is largely authority-based then the assessment difficulty is likely to be exacerbated. However, if a spirit of consultation and co-operation is achieved, then students may experience no difficulty in their core trainers being involved in personal development group work. One of the things which can help considerably is for the personal development group facilitators to show willingness to be participants in the personal development process within the group. This also models the fact that personal development is an on-going concern reaching far beyond basic training.

## PERSONAL JOURNALS

The BAC Course Recognition Scheme guidelines specifically require recognized courses to 'ensure that students maintain a "personal record" which monitors their own self-development' (BAC, 1990, p. 5). This is an unusual criterion because it is structural in nature: the Course Recognition Scheme is actually dictating, albeit in broad terms, a *method* by which the self-development should be monitored.

It is generally recognized that the real value of this personal record is that it is a place where the trainee 'speaks' to herself or himself, even about those important issues which they would find difficult to take to other parts of the course. With the content of journals being as private as this, trainers are naturally reluctant to assess the written work or even to demand that it be submitted for perusal by tutors.

It is possible to make regular use of the journal without demanding that its contents be laid open. In individual tutorials with a personal tutor or in small support groups students may be invited to use their recent entries in the personal journal to explore any aspects of their monitoring of self-development which they choose. In this way a regular focus is kept on the maintenance of the personal journal and yet the student is also given control over what is disclosed.

As a training course progresses, students may be invited, though seldom required, to engage in regular journal exchanges within a small support group. Once again, the emphasis must be on the student's power to control her or his disclosures. If that power is taken away, then the danger is that the student will reduce the important personal content of the journal, hence diminishing its value as a monitor of her or his development.

## OTHER CONTRIBUTIONS TO SELF-DEVELOPMENT

Numerous other parts of courses contribute to self-development. For example, some courses emphasize that the training period is one in which the trainee might usefully explore the *extension of his or her life experience*. In other words, the student would be encouraged, supported and helped to monitor efforts they might be making, for example, to become more familiar with different sub-cultures; to put themselves into contact with an otherwise feared group; or actively to experiment with alternative ways of relating in an effort to break inappropriate or inadequate habits. The personal development group is often the focus for encouraging, supporting and monitoring the course member's extension of their life experience and the power of such experimentation influences not only the individual student but also the other people in the group. It can be very moving, for example, to listen to a trainee who, having identified racist attitudes within herself, actively puts herself into the situation of working in a voluntary information and counselling service within a predominantly Pakistani community or the male trainee who bravely contracted himself into 20 weekly sessions in a men's group because he had a fear of men.

Some courses even see relevant self-development opportunities in the large course *community meetings*, although these may not appear to carry much self-development opportunity since there are so many people involved. These large meetings, particularly if they are relatively unstructured, create very different social contexts than smaller groups which can more easily develop norms to create stability and safety. At times this very difficult and unpredictable large gathering resembles more a microcosm of diverse society than a comfortable training context and can reach parts of the self which are untouched by other means. Furthermore, such groups present a larger forum for trainees who have reached the point of 'going public' with an element of self-awareness or self-change. This self-development use of the large group is more fully described in Mearns (1994).

Opportunities for self-development may be offered through structured experiential exercises primarily designed to encourage students to focus on specific aspects of personal growth. This model of human relationships and personal growth training assumes that although spontaneous experiences within a group setting may be valuable in terms of expanding awareness and emotional freedom, as much personal growth and solid, transferrable learning may result from carefully structured experiences, designed to focus on individual behaviour, constructive feedback, processing and psychological integration (Pfeiffer and Jones, 1973).

The range of self-development activities is considerable and appropriately reflects the diversity of theoretical models of counselling. Important in any course designer's mind should be the concordance between the self-development approaches and the core theoretical model of the course.

## THE SPIRIT OF SELF-DEVELOPMENT

Self-development in counselling training may be approached by one student with an open spirit of exploration – with a keenness to learn new things about self and to share these with others. Another student may approach the whole area as a threat, keeping herself or himself as closed as possible and existing under a cloud which carries the constant threat of 'being found out' as inadequate, ineffectual, or even evil. The spirit with which the staff approach the whole area of self-development and the model of openness or otherwise which they provide will influence the norm which is developed among the trainees. But people vary – indeed one person may vary over time or from one issue to another, being open to some and closed to others. Such is the nature of this work and of counsellor training, which touches the parts that other educational experiences do not reach!

# NINE

# Client work

In this chapter, we will consider the important subject of trainees' work with clients. In particular, we will discuss the concept of trainee readiness to see clients; counselling placements and the issues related to trainees being on placement; issues to do with clients; and issues concerning trainees reporting on their client work.

In many ways, client work is, in our view, the most important element of professional counsellor training. If such courses did not require trainees to see clients, it would be like a driving school not requiring a learner driver actually to drive a car on the open road. So much of counsellor training would be meaningless without client work: skills training would lose its purpose, there would be nothing to supervise and the core theoretical model would appear to be some nebulous framework without practical applications. This is not to say that courses without client work do not have their merit – they do, but they are more properly regarded as courses *about* counselling rather than professional training *in* counselling.

Having made the point emphatically that client work is the *sine qua non* of professional counsellor training courses, let us begin our discussion by considering the issue of trainee readiness to see clients.

## READINESS TO SEE CLIENTS

It is unrealistic to expect trainees without previous training or c~~ounselling~~ selling experience to start seeing clients as soon as the cours~~e is~~ begun. This leads to the questions: when are trainees ready ~~to see~~ clients and how is this to be assessed? We will concentrate criteria for readiness here and discuss assessment methods in Chapter 12.

## The core theoretical model

Before seeing clients trainees need to have a working knowledge of the core model, especially its mode of practice and reasons for its major interventions. They do not need to understand all the subtleties of a core theoretical model to begin to practise it. Trainers, then, need to give a lot of thought concerning which theoretical and practical aspects of the core model require to be presented and fully understood before trainees start seeing clients. An example of this kind of assessment for one core theoretical model (Rational Emotive Behaviour Therapy) is available in Dryden (1995b).

## Knowledge of client psychopathology

The profession of counselling has been criticized for not distinguishing between ordinary unhappiness and severely disturbed mental states (Persaud, 1993). Certainly, it is not yet a requirement that BAC-recognized courses have to provide teaching input which helps trainees to identify the signs that clients are severely disturbed and need psychiatric rather than counselling help. However, it might be argued that this is important information which trainees need to have at their fingertips before they see clients. It may also be helpful if trainees have a working knowledge of psychotropic medication since some of their clients are likely to be on prescribed drugs.

Counter-arguments might make the point that it is, in practice, difficult to give a new trainee *sufficient* knowledge of psychopathology, including medication, so early in the training and that this issue might better be handled either by careful assessment interviews with prospective clients or by close supervision of the student's early client work.

## Counselling skills

Carkhuff (1969) has written about the importance of counsellors offering their clients at least a minimum level of 'facilitative functioning'. If they offer any less then they are in danger of being ineffective with their clients or, worse, of doing them harm. Trainers can usefully apply this concept to skills training and specify the minimum level of skilfulness that trainees need to demonstrate in working with each other before they are deemed ready to see clients. It is important that trainees understand what this minimum level is at the outset so that they can (a) understand what they need to aim for in skills training; (b) assess their own progress;

and (c) judge the fairness of the assessment of their counselling skills. The skills at which trainees need to demonstrate a minimum level of competence will, of course, depend on the core theoretical model that underpins the course.

## Self-development

The selection procedures described in Chapter 5 include assessment of the applicant's self-development and readiness for training. If an applicant showed a level of self-development which made it inappropriate that they should work with clients, then they would not be selected for the training. However, reality can differ from theory and early in the training it may become apparent that one or two students have such difficulties regarding their self-development that they should not be practising. These difficulties may have been missed in selection or they may have been dormant and aroused by the early parts of the training experience. In either case, the responsibility of the trainers, in dialogue with the student, is, at the very least, to delay the start of counselling practice and perhaps to consider whether it is appropriate for training to continue at that time. This problem may also arise in the case of students who are not *beginning* practice but are continuing long-standing voluntary counselling work. In these cases the counselling agency needs to be included in the dialogue.

## COUNSELLING PLACEMENTS

## Counselling 'placements' and counselling 'opportunities'

A counselling placement provides trainees first and foremost with an opportunity to see clients. However, it also allows trainees to work in an organizational setting, be a part of a team and participate in some or most of the developmental activities that are offered to trained counsellors. The term 'placement' implies that the training course has some responsibility for 'placing' the student in that practice context. This section deals with the various responsibilities in relation to such placements, but it should be noted that many and sometimes most students on a training course have what might be termed 'counselling opportunities' rather than 'counselling placements'. Usually these counselling opportunities are in the context of the trainee's long-standing work with a voluntary counselling agency or in regard to their paid employment with a social work office or community care project. The main responsibility of the course in relation to students' counselling opportunities is to ensure that the context offers appropriate practice experience. With counselling 'placements' on the other hand, the course has the additional responsibilities discussed below.

## The match between student and placement agency

One issue that needs to be considered with respect to counselling placements concerns the match between the student and the placement agency. There are two kinds of matching: core model matching and personal matching. As we discussed in Chapter 3, it is ideal if students have a counselling placement at an agency which shares the core theoretical model of the course. At the very least, staff at a placement agency should not be overtly or covertly critical of the trainee's core model. If they are, then the match between student and placement agency may become untenable.

The second kind of matching is more personal. We believe that trainees need to get a sense that the placement agency will provide them with an opportunity for enhancing their learning and will allow them to be themselves. We also believe that the agency needs to determine whether or not the student is right for the agency. Thus, a period of mutual appraisal is usually carried out before a trainee and a placement agency make a commitment to one another. This used to be a fairly relaxed process. Now there is a dearth of good training placements and a glut of eager trainees looking for them. Nevertheless, unless there is a good reason to the contrary, trainees should not be unilaterally assigned to a placement; nor should placements be pressured into taking a trainee whom they do not want or have not interviewed. BAC has produced a useful information sheet on these issues (Coate, 1994).

## The relationship between the course, the student and the placement agency

The success of a training placement depends, in part, on the quality of the three-way relationship between the course, the student and the placement agency. In turn, this relationship depends upon what agreement is made between all three parties concerning their responsibilities during the placement. Unless such an agreement is made, there is a danger that unspoken expectations will not be met, a situation which is a breeding ground for dissatisfaction and resentment.

In working towards this agreement courses will be aware that the outcome must be one which brings advantages to all three parties involved. Since counselling training courses are rarely subsidized for placements by grant aid in the way that social work training courses receive support, it is not simply a matter of 'buying' the co-operation of the counselling agency. Realistically, the work which the student is undertaking must be of value in itself to the agency in order to compensate for the time they will spend on administration, student support and communicating with the training course.

In its negotiation with the placement agency the course will want to reach an agreement which ensures those conditions which it regards as fundamental and as many others which it would see as desirable.

It is important that the student plays an active part in forming this agreement. It is too easy for the student's voice to be lost as representatives from the course and the agency discuss their expectations of each other and their requirements of the student. Thus, the student's own expectations and requirements of the placement need to be heard, discussed and agreed before the placement begins.

The following are some of the issues which may be discussed in the formation of this three-way agreement.

- the amount of client work which the student is expected to undertake in the agency
- the type of clients which the student should or should not work with
- whether or not the placement agency is expected to provide supervision
- clarification on the other supervision (individual and/or group) which the student is receiving
- confidentiality requirements of the agency and how this affects supervision outside the agency
- whether tape-recording of client work is to be permitted (subject, of course, to the agreement of the individual client)
- how the issue of clinical responsibility for the student's work is to be handled
- the nature of contact between the placement agency and the course during the placement
- whether a course tutor is expected to visit the student on placement and, if so, the frequency and purpose of such visits
- how the issue of responsibility is to be handled among the three parties. For example, one agreement might expect the placement agency and the student to do everything they can to sort out differences and difficulties, with contact only being made with the training course in the event of differences and difficulties persisting
- procedures in the event of the placement agency having concern about the quality or ethical nature of the student's work
- procedures to follow in the event of the course developing reservations about the student's suitability to practise.

Courses and placement agencies will vary widely in their expec‑ tions on the above issues. For example, some courses will feel it is their responsibility to maintain considerable responsibility fr work of the student during placement. Such a course is likely to want to be highly interventionist in its relationship with student and agency. Another course, perhaps reflective of a different core theoretical model, might wish to shift the balance of responsibility in order to give more emphasis to the student feeling responsible for his or her work in the agency. In this example the agreement which might be drawn up would allow for the student and the agency to negotiate their relationship more directly together, only involving the course on particularly important or difficult issues.

## The contract

Whatever the details of the agreement formed between the course, the student and the agency, the parties might consider putting the agreement in writing. This represents a formal contract between the three parties involved. Any changes to this contractual agreement would then need to be discussed, preferably in a three-way meeting between the student, a course staff member and a representative from the placement.

A major frustration for students on placement concerns being suddenly asked to do something extra by the agency that has not been subject to an agreement. This sometimes happens because someone at the agency does not know of the conditions of the contractual agreement. Consequently, it is useful if the contractual agreement (and any subsequent amendments) is made available to all relevant parties at the placement so that the chances that the student is given extra, uncontracted work are minimized.

This may sound very legalistic, but if it is done in the right spirit with all parties wanting the placement to be a success then the clarity it brings to the placement experience for all concerned outweighs any negative connotations that a written contract may have for some people.

While we have dwelled on what might go wrong when a student is on placement, we wish to end this section by emphasizing that a well-managed placement can provide a tremendously important source of support for students and can be instrumental to the development of the student's confidence as a counsellor and their emerging professional identity.

## ISSUES RELATING TO CLIENTS

The BAC guidelines for course recognition say that students 'must have opportunities for substantial and regular ... counselling work with real clients (i.e. in addition to any counselling practice with fellow students). ... Client work must be understood by both the student and the client as "counselling" rather than "befriending", "supporting", or any other kind of relationship which uses counselling skills but is not "counselling" as such' (BAC, 1990, p. 5).

Thus, only formal counselling with real clients is accepted as client work on professional counsellor training courses. Since this is in line with professional training in other disciplines, it can be regarded as accepted practice. But how much of such formal counselling is required? The following BAC course recognition guideline (BAC, 1990, pp. 22–3) addresses this issue:

> Part-time counselling training courses frequently expect students to undergo 200, 300 or 400 hours of *supervised practice* during training. However, for one-year full-time courses, such targets are difficult to reach. For this reason we regard a notional 100 hours of supervised practice as a minimum during the training period. However, once again, a figure such as this should not be taken as a simple target to be met. The CRG investigating panel might still regard the 100 hours as insufficient if it did not give the student experience of working with a range of clientele. Equally, in certain circumstances, the panel might regard marginally less than 100 hours as sufficient, but the course would need to present an argument to justify this.

Let us consider in greater depth some of the issues that are contained in this statement.


## CLIENTS HAVE TO BE SEEN DURING THE COURSE RATHER THAN AFTER THE COURSE HAS FINISHED

As we have stated many times in this book, professional counsellor training involves a number of *interactive* basic elements. As such, this means that client work has to occur while the course is running so that trainees can benefit from the other elements of the course while they are in progress. However, there are non-BAC-recognized courses which allow trainees to start seeing clients after all the other elements of the course (apart from supervision) have finished. We are unhappy with this practice since it means that students' supervised client work cannot inform their work in the other elements of the course since the latter are over before they start seeing clients. While there is nothing in the BAC recognition guidelines specifically on this point, this practice does not encourage students to be reflective practitioners, which is a major objective of professional counsellor training (see Chapter 2).

THE MINIMUM FIGURE OF 100 HOURS WAS SET TO ACCOMMODATE
FULL-TIME COUNSELLING COURSES INTO THE RECOGNITION
SCHEME

Since the minimum figure of 100 supervised hours of client work
was established with one-year, full-time courses very much in mind,
we wonder if this figure is large enough for part-time courses which
might span three years. For example, on a part-time, three-year counselling course, even allowing for the fact that students may not start
seeing clients until the second year of the course, such students may
only need to see one client a week to meet the guideline, while their
full-time colleagues would have to see five clients a week in the second
and third terms of their course.

Also, there is no guidance in the BAC recognition guidelines on
how many different clients are to be seen. We predict that the entire
issue of client hours will have to be reconsidered by the BAC Courses
Recognition Group before long.

THE RANGE OF CLIENTS SEEN IS AN IMPORTANT FACTOR

While the guidelines point out that a range of clients seen is an
important factor it gives no further guidance on what constitutes a range
of clients, whether or not clients from different populations should be
seen, whether or not students are allowed to see fee-paying, private
clients, etc. These issues will probably need to be addressed before
long as part of a broader discussion concerning what constitutes
acceptable client work on professional counsellor training courses.

## Other issues

Let us now consider other important issues with respect to clients
and client work.

SHOULD CLIENTS BE ASSESSED BEFORE BEING REFERRED
TO TRAINEES?

One view on this issue is that it is helpful at the beginning of
a placement for students to see clients who are not too disturbed
(e.g. those with chronic problems). This means that someone in the
placement agency needs to assess clients specifically for beginning
trainees. Ideal beginning clients would be articulate, well-motivated
people who have concerns that are not severe. Later on in the placement,
once students' confidence has increased, such prior assessment of clients
may be dispensed with and students allowed to take direct referrals. In
general, trainees who have had prior practice before starting the course
may need to be protected less than those without such experience.

Another view on this issue is that trainees are individuals and some may benefit more without this early career protection. An alternative way to proceed is to forgo client assessment but to invest more in the supervision available to the counsellors-in-training so that they have extra support when working with clients who prove testing for them. An example of this procedure is detailed in Chapter 10. This alternative policy also allows for the fact that many of the difficulties which counsellors-in-training encounter with clients are not simply to do with the nature of the client's psychopathology but relate to what the client represents for the trainee.

Any decision on assessment must consider the position of clients. However, this is not a straightforward matter. Although the employment of an assessment interview may appear to offer more protection for clients, it can also be a dreadful experience for a vulnerable client when they are expected to tell their story once again to an assessor with whom they will have no continuing relationship.

SHOULD THE TRAINEE'S CLIENT LOAD GRADUALLY INCREASE?

There is a logic in gradually increasing the trainee's client load during training, especially if she or he has not had substantive counselling experience before starting the course. However, individual differences again need to be respected. Some trainees would prefer to start with the same client load as they intend to carry throughout the placement. Another consideration related to this is the minimum number of clients which the trainee should see at the start of their client work. Here, we might caution against the logical presumption that working with *one* client is the easiest way to begin. When a counsellor-in-training has only one client the counsellor can easily become vulnerable to the 'ups and downs' of the individual therapeutic process – alternately feeling satisfaction and despair as the client's progress appears positive or stalled. Trainees who are working with more clients are less vulnerable to the oscillations of individual clients.

## KEEPING A LOG OF CLIENT WORK

The BAC course recognition guidelines state that: 'Details of the client work should be included in a "professional log" which the student maintains and presents at assessment' (BAC, 1990, p. 5).

Here is an example of the instructions that one two-year, part-time course gives to its students concerning the keeping of the professional log.

1. The practice requirement for the course is that you conduct

a minimum of 300 counselling sessions over two years. You are further required to keep a log of these sessions.

2. For each session, you should include details of the client's process and your understanding of this process, your interventions, the quality of your relationship with the client and what you learned about yourself as a counsellor. You should make clear throughout how the core theoretical model informed your understanding of this material.

3. You should structure your log in such a way that your sessions with each client are organized sequentially. You should make clear your understanding of the process nature of counselling for each client.

4. You should not include the client's name or any obvious identifying details in your log. We suggest that you refer to each client by an initial (but not the client's real initials) or by a number.

5. Your professional log will be assessed at the end of each year and this assessment will count towards your final assessment.

6. The following assessment criteria will be used:

    6.1. The depth of your understanding of your client's process.

    6.2. The relevance of your therapeutic interventions.

    6.3. The depth of your understanding of the dynamics of the client–counsellor relationship.

    6.4. The depth of your understanding of counselling as a process.

    6.5. The depth of your learning with respect to your own contribution to the counselling process.

    6.6. The extent to which you have made relevant use of the core theoretical model to inform your understanding of your work with clients.

Other instructions and assessment criteria might make greater use of concepts that are central to the course's core theoretical model. Also, some courses ask students to make a summary statement at the end of each year concerning their view of their development as trainee counsellors.

In addition to the professional log, some recognized courses ask students at the end of their placement to write an account of their placement experience. This might include their reflections on the organizational dynamics of the agency and the influence that these dynamics might have on their own client work in particular and on client work carried out in the agency in general. This latter task would be informed by the theoretical material on social systems and the ways that these affect counselling practice as well as by the core theoretical model.

As we noted earlier in this chapter, all client work has to be supervised. In the next chapter we discuss supervision in the context of professional counsellor training.

# TEN
# Supervision

The BAC course recognition booklet (BAC, 1990) describes three functions which should be served by supervision:

helping the student to integrate theory with practice and to develop competent practice (the *training* function);
maintaining the student's personal and professional well-being with respect to client work (the *supportive* function);
affording a degree of protection for the student's clients (the *managerial* function). (p. 5)

However supervision is arranged during training, these three functions need to be met. Coincidentally, there are three main forms of supervision and while those three forms emphasize different functions they will each contribute to all three functions.

## COUNSELLING AGENCY SUPERVISION

Understandably, the main concern of agency supervision is to serve the *managerial* function by affording a degree of protection to the client and also to the agency. The agency supervisor monitors the counsellor's way of working to ensure that risks are not being taken and clients are not being abused. The supervisor has the power to intervene directly in the counsellor's work in order to protect the client or the agency.

Although the agency supervision is principally designed to meet the managerial function it will also contribute to the student's personal and professional well-being with respect to the work. Indeed, some agency supervisors create such a good relationship with the trainee that the latter is more aware of the supportive function being met than the managerial function. Agency supervision may also feed the training function, though further supervision is usually necessary to ensure sufficiency in that regard, particularly if the agency supervision is not consistent with the core theoretical model of the training.

The issue of responsibility is significant when considering the extent to which counselling agency supervision is likely to serve supportive and training functions as well as the managerial. Because the counselling agency supervisor is principally responsible *to* the client and the agency, he or she exerts a responsibility *for* the work of the supervisee, tending, almost inevitably, to take a 'deficiency' rather than a 'potentiality' model of working with respect to the counsellor's development. The consequence of this role conflict between the supervisor's principal responsibility to the client/agency and secondary responsibility to the counsellor can be the counsellor's experiencing a lack of safety and beginning to hide some of his or her practice from the supervisor. It is for this reason that the BAC Code of Ethics and Practice for Counsellors (BAC, 1993b) declares that line-management counselling supervision on its own is insufficient: a more confidential supervision support is also required to maintain the counsellor's personal and professional well-being. Occasionally that individual supervision is paid for by the counselling agency, for example, many student counsellors have won the battle to have their individual supervision regarded as allowable staff development. However, in too many cases the counsellor is left to engage his or her own individual supervisor.

## INDIVIDUAL PERSONAL SUPERVISION

The main function met by individual personal supervision is the *supportive* function – the provision of a confidential consultancy relationship in which the counsellor can raise his or her most difficult questions pertaining to their counselling practice in the knowledge that they will be protected by the confidentiality of that relationship. Insofar as the confidential relationship of individual personal supervision helps the counsellor to maintain his or her professional well-being with respect to client work it also indirectly serves the managerial function of protecting the client. Indeed, it might be argued that the client is afforded better protection through this individual personal care of the counsellor rather than through a form of line-management supervision which seeks to monitor the counsellor's performance but may pressure the practitioner into a state of hiding. Once again, this is the thinking behind the insistence that at least some of the supervision provided should not be of the line-management variety. Comparisons between these two forms of supervision would also be relevant for the social work profession which has a norm of line-management agency supervision but not a history of confidential individual personal supervision. Interestingly, a number of social workers employ their own counselling supervisor to provide the supportive function.

Individual personal supervision may also fulfil a training function. Indeed, courses vary on how much they use individual supervision to provide that training function. Some courses prefer the individual supervision to be relatively independent of the course in order to ensure the more confidential relationship necessary for support, while others involve the individual supervisor quite fully in the course, with regular briefings and guidance on the concepts to be raised in supervision at particular times. Courses attempting to integrate the individual supervision in this way may even involve the supervisor in assessment, perhaps requiring a report on the counsellor's practice. Of course, the closer the individual supervision is brought to the course the greater the danger that the special confidential relationship is lost and the supportive function endangered.

An important question for training courses is who should provide the individual supervision. The course may opt for that supervision to be provided by course tutors, although it can be argued that this obviously loses the independence and confidentiality which might be important to the trainee if he or she is to use the supervision fully in a supportive way. As far as the criterion guidelines for BAC course recognition is concerned there is no definite rule against using tutors but courses tend to be encouraged to make the individual supervision more independent. However, as is often the case with the Course Recognition Scheme, courses are encouraged to make a case for their own practices.

It is more common for a course to compile a list of 'approved' supervisors, perhaps also including the possibility of vetting other candidates put forward by individual trainees. A major criterion in the selection of supervisors for such a list is the concordance between the core theoretical model of the supervisor and that of the course. There is little which is more troublesome for a trainee than having training in one core model and supervision in another. Just one illustration of this difficulty was a trainee on a Person-Centred course who was having individual supervision with a Gestalt supervisor. Although the supervisor was very supportive of Person-Centred theory, she was not trained at depth in that approach. Every time there arose any element of therapeutic 'stuckness' the trainee would be encouraged to work in a way which was characteristic of Gestalt intervention. The result was that the trainee never got over that hurdle in her development as a Person-Centred counsellor where she might be expected to check her experience with the client and perhaps explore the nature and dynamics of the apparent stuckness itself. For an experienced professional counsellor, supervision by someone from another discipline can be stimulating but the difference is that the experienced counsellor has already developed a coherent framework for mediating her work whereas the trainee is struggling to construct that framework.

Having provided a list of approved supervisors, most courses allow trainees to come to their own contract with the supervisor. This makes the relationship identical to that which the professional counsellor has with his or her individual supervisor, who is an employee selected and paid by the counsellor. The contract, then, is between the trainee and the individual supervisor, thus making the supervisor principally responsible to the trainee rather than to the course. Many courses insert one or two caveats into that independence, perhaps stipulating guidelines for the *amount* and *regularity* of the supervision and often inserting an exceptional clause into the confidential relationship by expecting the supervisor to make contact with the course in the event of the trainee being involved in unethical or incompetent practice. In inserting this clause there is always a risk that the course will lose the important safety of the confidential relationship, but it is difficult for courses totally to relinquish responsibility in this regard. In any case, a professional counselling supervisor might find unethical or incompetent practice to be sufficient cause for breaking confidentiality. (See BAC, 1988.)

## GROUP SUPERVISION

As well as contributing to the course member's feeling of well-being and in that way serving the supportive function, group supervision mainly exists as a forum for the *training* function, helping the student to integrate theory and skills with practice. While other parts of the course will start with theoretical issues and show their relevance to practice, group supervision starts with the concurrent practice of trainees and relates that practice to theory as well as to skill development.

Although group supervision contributes to the supportive and managerial functions on its own, it is usually insufficient to ensure adequate cover of those functions. A course may devote considerable time to group supervision, often 20 per cent of the course time or more. That time is well spent because, as far as training needs are concerned, the trainee is learning even when another student's practice is the focus of attention. The reason why group supervision is usually insufficient to meet the supportive and managerial functions in full is the simple fact that the size of the group can mean that each trainee is not receiving sufficient attention for the meeting of those functions. Group size varies considerably: many psychodynamic training courses in particular are to be commended on group sizes of three or four, which allows each student to receive considerable attention to his or her work. However, the economics of training more often means group sizes of between six and nine, which is acceptable if the central function of the group supervision is seen as training and the supportive and managerial functions are being met elsewhere.

Group supervision may begin *before* counselling practice commences on a training course. Obviously the focus during that early phase cannot be on the trainees' actual counselling practice, but instead the group can use the members' video skills practice work as the starting point for supervision. This combination of group supervision and skills practice works well to create a spirit of openness about the work. Having become used to analysing video skills practice it then becomes a smaller step to analyse audiotapes of each other's actual counselling practice. As mentioned earlier, in addition to the direct learning of each trainee resulting from looking at his or her own work, there is a strong vicarious learning element which arises from examining the issues in the work of fellow students. This process involves each student relating to the concerns of another as though it were a 'critical incident' into which the trainee projects himself or herself and asks the question 'What would *I* do if I were the counsellor in this situation?' Listening to other trainees present their counselling work can help people in the group to identify and articulate problems and issues in their own work. This can be particularly valuable since beginning counsellors-in-training often experience similar problems and difficulties.

## APPROACHES TO SUPERVISION

The aim of supervision is to monitor the counsellor's practice and use that to further his or her learning. It follows that the closer the supervision can get to the actual counselling practice then the more relevant and immediate might be the learning which results. Logically, then, we must consider the possibility of the supervisor being present and giving feedback to the counsellor during the actual counselling session. In fact, this model of supervision exists and is relatively common in family therapy, where the supervisor may be seated behind a one-way vision screen and able to communicate with the counsellor via 'bug in the ear' technology. Although many counsellors would shriek with alarm at such an interventionist approach to counselling supervision, this technique is powerful in the immediacy of feedback which it permits.

Other models of supervision provide decreasing degrees of *contact* with the actual counselling work of the trainee. If the supervisor or supervision group view a videotape of the counsellor's actual work then they are very close to the fullness of that work although somewhat behind it temporally. Using audiotapes of actual counselling sessions is slightly less full in terms of information than videotapes but still powerful in bringing the actual counselling session into direct contact with the supervisor or group.

Thorough supervision of a trainee's work can only be done through analysing videotapes or audiotapes of actual counselling practice. Any other method fails to bring the actual counselling work into consideration by the supervisor. The strange paradox in counselling and counsellor training is that the vast bulk of supervision does *not* deal with the above direct methods but relies almost exclusively on the second-hand accounts of the counselling process given by the counsellor or trainee counsellor. The conventional reliance on this practice is questioned by Godden (1994). Any objective pedagogical critique would question the reliance in supervision on second-hand rather than direct accounts. It can be interesting for the trainee counsellor to discuss his or her views on the client's experience in counselling but the degree to which that second-hand account actually mirrors the reality of counselling must be questioned. Counsellors, like all human beings, have a tendency and a need to create a coherent picture of events – a picture whose coherence is largely determined by the counsellor's own valued constructs. When listening to lengthy case discussion during supervision the inescapable query is 'How different would be the client's account of this work?'

The fact that most supervision relies on a second-hand account of proceedings does not mean that it is of little value to the counsellor. A skilled supervisor can invite the counsellor to question his or her construction of the client's experience, actually helping the counsellor to be aware of a range of possibilities rather than being narrowed down to one. As an example of the importance of this influence by the supervisor, take the case of the counsellor who presumed that the various experiences a particular client was presenting represented indirect evidence that the client had been abused as a child and was unconsciously denying that experience. Once a presumption like this is formed it is difficult for the trainee counsellor to avoid influencing the client towards considering that possibility. However, that may be a potentially dangerous influence upon a client who is already vulnerable to the constructions of others. Fortunately, the supervisor was able to help the counsellor to develop a healthy scepticism about the presumption by actively considering a range of alternative explanations. In due course the client identified her earlier experiences as systematic emotional, but not sexual, abuse.

As well as helping the supervisee to take a broader perspective on the client, supervision can also encourage the counsellor-in-training to consider her or his *own* behaviour, becoming aware of and understanding their experience and reasons for acting as they do. Furthermore, the supervisor can help the counsellor to consider the nature and evolution of the *relationship* with the client, at least from the counsellor's own perspective.

Although supervision based on the counsellor's second-hand account of the work is limited in the knowledge it can offer about the client it is still an important means by which the counsellor can remain open to the client's experience and actively monitor the counsellor's own involvement in the work.

## SUPERVISION SHOULD BE BOTH REGULAR AND SUFFICIENT

As a guideline for *regularity*, the BAC course recognition booklet suggests: 'Students should have some form of regular contact with their supervisor every week or fortnight, and during that time to at least have the opportunity to present any problematic aspect of their work with current clients' (BAC, 1990, p. 23). This guideline is usually fairly easy to meet since courses tend to have arrangements in place for the trainee to have contact with both a supervision group and also their own individual supervisor. The importance of regularity is simply to ensure that the student has some immediate place to take difficulties in his or her work.

The guideline on *sufficiency* is more difficult to define in terms of number of hours. It is best stated functionally:

It is not easy to give guidance on the minimum amount of supervision time which students should receive. Basically the course should ensure that a student is receiving sufficient supervision to maintain the well-being of the student and their clients. (BAC, 1990, p. 23)

For a number of years both the individual accreditation and course recognition schemes of BAC endeavoured to operate the sufficiency criterion as stated above. However, it became obvious that it was necessary to define an absolute minimum amount of required supervision. The individual accreditation scheme set that minimum at one and a half hours per month. The course recognition scheme accepted that figure but set an *additional* guideline which would increase the amount of necessary supervision above that minimum if the trainee's counselling caseload was particularly high:

This is likely to demand around 1 hour individual supervision for every 8 client counselling hours. Certainly, it is difficult to imagine a ratio of worse than 1: 10 being sufficient for a student in training. This guideline may imply more supervision than the 1½ hours per month required in BAC accreditation applications but it is our belief that students require more supervision than experienced practitioners. (BAC, 1990, p. 23)

This additional criterion makes no difference to the minimum amount of supervision required if the student's caseload is less than three client hours per week but it copes with the situation of the trainee who is doing six hours counselling per week and needs much more supervision than the accreditation minimum of one and a half hours per month.

In computing this sufficiency guideline the cover offered to each trainee in group supervision relates to the number of people in the group. A small supervision group of three people offers much more individual attention than does a group of nine. The course recognition guidelines provide an example to illustrate the combination of group supervision and individual supervision:

If a course demands 2 hours individual supervision per month, plus 8 hours in a group of eight students, these figures combine to a total of 3 hours of 'individual equivalent' supervision per month. In normal circumstances this could be regarded as 'sufficient' supervision cover for a caseload of 24 counselling hours in that month. (BAC, 1990, p. 24)

In many ways it is a pity that the sufficiency guidelines have had to be defined as tightly as above. It is necessary simply because the basic notion that the counsellor or trainee counsellor needed sufficient supervision to maintain their own well-being and that of their clients was interpreted in grossly varying ways by different agencies and courses. Accreditation applications were being received where the counsellor was receiving one hour individual equivalent supervision per year! Hence, it became necessary to give a more precise guideline.

The danger in this precise guideline is that it still may not cover those situations where the trainee counsellor is involved in particularly demanding work where to maintain the well-being of the student and the client requires much more intensive supervision. The following case study illustrates a situation where the BAC-recognized course involved had to offer the student considerably more supervision support.

As a counsellor-in-training, Nazreen was highly competent, but it became apparent in group supervision that work with two of her clients was particularly demanding. The work with both clients was progressing well with Nazreen functioning as well as could be expected, but the pressure of the work was felt more by Nazreen than would have been the case for a more experienced worker. There is no easy solution in an instance such as this. The first consideration is the protection of the client. It was judged that simply referring these two clients to a more experienced counsellor would by no means offer 'protection' to the clients, who had invested considerable amounts in their relationships with Nazreen. Instead, it was decided that the best way to offer protection to the clients was to increase the support offered to Nazreen. This was done initially through extra individual sessions with her group supervisor and later by the course paying for additional support from her individual supervisor. The result not only offered safety for the clients but considerable development for Nazreen as a counsellor.

This case study represents a more accurate reflection of the sufficiency criterion than any guideline depicting a specific number of hours. The essential ingredient is to provide enough supervision to sustain the psychological health of the counsellor-in-training so that he or she may, in turn, offer a healthy relationship to the client. In extreme cases that may even mean offering a supervision to counselling ratio of 1:1 in the case of a trainee working with a client who is particularly difficult. Although that appears to be a huge investment of resources, it also tends to have a large dividend not only for the client, but also for the trainee because supervision is rich in the resources it offers not only in terms of personal support, but also in self-understanding, not to mention the power it has in helping theory to come to life in the context of practice.

Where a training course attends to supervision in ways which are sufficiently flexible to meet widely varying individual need on the part of students it is also offering an important model for *professional development*, implicitly giving the message to students that in the counselling profession we take seriously the need to maintain the quality of our work. The next chapter looks in more detail at aspects of professional development and how a positive attitude towards these can be engendered by a training course.

# ELEVEN
# Professional development

## WHAT IS PROFESSIONAL DEVELOPMENT?

The term 'professional' can be used very broadly to refer to anyone who is reliable and trustworthy. According to Windt *et al.* (1991), someone with professional status has expertise, authority, social importance, autonomy and self-regulation, commitment and reward. Dooley (1994) suggests that in addition to 'the development of technical skills and expertise, to be granted professional status requires significant additional steps: the expertise must be unique to the profession; there must be formal training; and there must be clear standards of conduct by which the public are protected' (p. 787). In this sense, all the theory training, skills work, counselling practice, supervision and even self-development might be deemed to be contributing towards the professional development of the counsellor-in-training. However, apart from these basic elements, there is also a special professional development curriculum encompassing all the things *around* the counsellor's work with the client. This curriculum includes everything the counsellor does to help make the work possible and to sustain its quality outside the actual skills of the counselling interaction. It encompasses, for instance, attention to the *context* of the work: ensuring the suitability of the work setting, being diligent over attendance and punctuality and, in general, being responsible *to* the client without taking responsibility *for* the client.

It is likely that a number of trainees will consider setting up in *private practice* for at least part of their livelihood at some time in their career. Consequently, part of the professional development curriculum will be to provide an opportunity to reflect on issues concerning private practice. These issues range from the practical (for example, selecting an office in which one is going to work; setting an appropriate fee and sliding scale of charges; developing a billing system and taking out business insurance) to the professional (for example, establishing and nurturing contacts with referral agents and agencies; marketing one's services as well as making relationships with other counsellors who are also in private practice). Students might be made aware of the emerging literature on counselling in private practice (for example, McMahon, 1993) and relevant journals (for example, *Psychotherapy in Private Practice*). An important dimension of professional development is considering issues which are controversial within the profession. The very notion of private practice is one such issue with many organizations and trainers disapproving of the concept. Professional development is achieved by engaging in, rather than avoiding, such debate.

More trainees will graduate to work within an *organizational setting* than in private practice. It is important, therefore, that trainees are helped to understand the dynamics of counselling within an institutional setting. Much can be gained from a simple comparison of the institutional settings within which students engage in counselling work during the course. For example, it is informative to compare the expectations on the counsellor in different settings: counselling within primary care, student counselling, counselling within an employee assistance programme and counselling within social work settings. Comparison of these different contexts allows the student to identify the various expectations which may impinge on his or her working, for example, expectations on the length of the working contract, the duration of a counselling session, an appropriate relationship with the client, the kind of referral which is deemed appropriate and whether there is implicit pressure upon the counsellor to take some responsibility *for* the client. Professional development in relation to working within an institution does not merely involve learning *about* institutions. It can also encompass considerable personal development associated with helping the counsellor-in-training to explore and come to terms with the personal issues involved in his or her relating with managers. The ingredients for difficulties within these relationships are numerous, including problems at the psychological level, such as transference, but also difficulties of a sociological nature, such as are created by the manager having a principal responsibility to the institution while the counsellor feels a predominance of responsibility to the client. Once again, this area is one which is ripe for debate and is best tackled in that open way.

Maintaining professional development entails the counsellor-in-training becoming an informed consumer of current *research*. Furthermore, in the current economic climate of increasing accountability and quality assurance many courses run workshops for students on how to evaluate their own work with clients. This may include the design and implementation of simple client evaluation or feedback forms. Counsellors-in-training need to become accountable for what they do and why they do it and this involves acquiring the skills to evaluate their own practice.

Professional development includes gaining some understanding of the *work of other professionals* in the mental health field. Some courses invite contributions from other professionals while others require students to go on agency visits to see and discuss the work of other helping professionals. At the very least courses may make use of the fact that within the student cohort there is typically a wealth of knowledge and experience of work in fields related to counselling.

Membership of a *professional body* such as the British Association for Counselling (BAC) is a relevant aspect of professional development insofar as that implies working within the prescribed ethical code and the opportunity to work towards accredited status with that body. Membership of an organization such as BAC brings other professional benefits, including the opportunity to attend the annual conference, to join one of the many specialist divisions or local groups and, through receipt of the journal, to keep up-to-date with changes and developments both within BAC and more generally in the counselling field within Britain and Europe.

Some professional counselling bodies regard the taking out of *indemnity insurance* as an aspect of ethical or professional responsibility. It is interesting that the BAC Code of Ethics and Practice for Counsellors (BAC, 1993b) requires that the counsellor *considers* his or her position with respect to indemnity insurance though it does not make a definite requirement for such insurance. That position fairly accurately reflects the profession, where there is unfinished debate about whether the holding of such insurance is really for the benefit of the client (Mearns, 1993a). Once again, the professional counsellor training course assists the trainee's professional development not by prescribing or proscribing the taking out of such insurance but by raising discussion on the issues involved.

Perhaps the most important topic pertaining to professional development concerns counsellor *stress and burn-out*. If trainees can establish healthy patterns of personal and professional self-care early in their counselling career they may become able to deal constructively with the stresses of counselling and prevent professional burn-out. It is easy for counselling trainees to develop the illusion that they are immune from the stress that accompanies one's work as a counsellor. Indeed, from the outset of training, many trainees believe that now they are entering the counselling profession they must not admit even to themselves that they are experiencing problems arising directly from their work as counsellors. This shame-based attitude can wreak havoc, not only later on in their career as counsellors, but also during training. Supervision and personal development groups are two important settings in which this issue of stress can be directly identified and explored and for this reason these activities are best facilitated by people who are brave enough to admit to their own stress as a counsellor and how that stress was managed. Recent texts offer explorations of counsellor stress and burn-out (Dryden, 1995a; Mearns, 1994).

One of the most interesting and important dimensions of counsellor training sometimes located within the professional development curriculum relates to the counsellor achieving a sociological perspective to his or her working. The counsellor must develop an awareness of the cultures and sub-cultures from which his or her clients are drawn so that their behaviour can be understood in relation to their cultural norms and values. Counsellors also need to be aware of the kinds of reality which they are creating in their work with clients. This notion of the *social construction of reality* is of crucial importance to understanding how behaviour which seems to be perfectly appropriate when viewed from within the counselling relationship may look quite different outside that reality. The vast majority of breaches of counselling ethics are a result of the counsellor's lack of awareness of the reality which he or she has socially constructed with a client and the gulf between that reality and outside perspectives. In many cases the counsellor is not knowingly behaving in an unethical fashion, but has become seduced by the reality he or she has constructed around the counselling relationship. We might illustrate this with the example of the counsellor who developed a habit with a particular client of ending each session by placing her hands on the top of the client's head. This had arisen in the relationship as a way in which the counsellor helped the client to develop the strength to continue her life for the coming week. Some years after this counselling relationship had ended and the spell of the special reality which had been created was broken, the client felt extremely angry at the thought that she had been 'seduced' into such a submissive role in this ritual. The counsellor was surprised at her former client's anger and genuinely did not appreciate that she had behaved unethically by mystifying the client with this 'laying-on-of-hands' ritual: when viewed from the counsellor's reality her motivation had been one of tremendous caring for the client and the desire to use all her faculties to the client's benefit. Counselling is an intense relationship in which the power is distributed unequally. These are the perfect ingredients for the social construction of a reality which may feel fine from inside the reality but could appear quite different when viewed from outside, either by other people or by the client at a later time. One of the most important areas for professional development is the counsellor developing a sociological perspective whereby he or she can view the reality they are creating with a client from various other perspectives including the current perspective of the client, the possible future perspective of the client and the perspectives of relevant outside persons. In this way the decisions taken by the counsellor are informed by a broader set of realities rather than by his or her own inclinations in the moment.

## ENCOURAGING PROFESSIONAL DEVELOPMENT

Some aspects of professional development will be *formally* addressed by the training course, including early consideration of the BAC Code of Ethics and Practice for Counsellors (1993b) before counselling practice commences. Although conventional wisdom demands this early attention to ethics, the students are likely to get much more from the exercise if it is reintroduced at some later stage once they have had the benefit of considerable practice. After some experience the ethical issues will be more meaningful for the students. Other formal professional development sessions may focus on social and cultural factors in counselling and also on the social construction of reality as well as early attention to the practicalities of organizing counselling practice and the importance of attention to boundaries. A typical, formal, professional development curriculum would include some of the following topics:

- selecting and contracting with a supervisor
- using tape recorders in counselling – practical and ethical issues
- personal safety and security for the counsellor
- writing case notes
- record-keeping, confidentiality and the law
- writing letters to clients
- developing a resource network
- making referrals
- introduction to the Code of Ethics
- case studies on ethical decision-making and problem-solving
- setting up in private practice
- advertising a counselling service
- dealing with client fees
- indemnity insurance
- setting up a counselling agency
- the counsellor as change agent within an organization
- monitoring and evaluating the competence of the counsellor – including quality assurance and clinical audit
- evaluation of client work outcomes
- understanding, interpreting and evaluating research reports
- individual counsellor accreditation and national registration
- national and international developments within the field
- nature and purpose of supervision after training
- counsellor stress and burn-out
- opportunities for further training
- professional development after basic training.

Formal sessions focusing on particular aspects of professional development have considerable value for both providing information and encouraging debate. However, an ever more powerful way of encouraging professional development is carefully to *integrate* dimensions of professionalism into the whole fabric of the training. So, for example, as well as giving a formal introduction to professional issues, course tutors will be ready to raise these as they become relevant within supervision and personal development groups. Furthermore, the training course itself can be regarded as a professional community, with staff modelling a consistent willingness to be responsible *to* participants without falling into the dependency culture of being responsible *for* the participant. In this regard, staff would be as diligent as trainers as they are as counsellors in their attendance, punctuality and preparedness for sessions as well as their attention to the detail of administration. The staff can further model the value they attach to professional development by regularly drawing students' attention to the latest issues in professional journals and discussing the relevance of some of the articles to their on-going training work. Even the difficult subject of the 'social construction of reality' can be brought to life by trainers willing to reflect upon themselves and encouraging students' reflections on the nature of the reality being created on the course itself. Each small group on the course, and also the whole course community meeting, will develop its own culture with norms being continually established and revised. Opening that process to discussion notably helps students learn about the social construction of reality but it also shares responsiblity for the on-going evaluation of the training course. Staff willingness to share that responsibility with trainee colleagues is, in itself, a powerful way to encourage the trainee's professional development.

Professional development is not complete at the end of a training course. It is important throughout to emphasize the on-going nature of professional development. Once again, that might be mirrored by the trainers' open attention to their own professional development, but that longer-term professional attitude is also encouraged in the trainee by helping him or her to become more expert in assessing strengths, weaknesses and needs for the future. Probably more than any other career training, counselling tends to *involve* students in their own monitoring and assessment because their longer-term professional development will depend on their ability to reflect upon their practice and identify their own needs. This takes us appropriately to a more detailed consideration of assessment in counsellor training.

# TWELVE
# Assessment

Assessment is sometimes regarded as synonymous with evaluation. However, we intend to treat assessment and evaluation as two quite separate and distinct activities. Assessment is concerned with the nature and quality of students' learning – their strengths and relative weaknesses, whereas evaluation is concerned with finding out about the effectiveness and quality of the course (Rowntree, 1987). The word evaluation is sometimes used generically to encompass the functions of both assessment and evaluation (BAC, 1990; Barnes, 1982). We think this is misleading. Although student assessment may be part of course evaluation, it is only a small part. It is for this reason we deal with assessment and evaluation in two separate chapters. This chapter is concerned with the assessment of students and the next chapter deals with the evaluation of courses.

Rowntree (1981, p. 178) identifies a number of reasons that are commonly put forward to justify assessment. These reasons include: to motivate students, to give feedback to students and staff, to establish and maintain standards, to prepare students for real-life practice and further education or training. Rowntree suggests that these boil down to two key functions. The first function is to use the knowledge gained from assessment to help teach students or help them to learn and the second is to use the knowledge to inform or report to others. The sort of people who would be interested in information about a student's qualifications and abilities as a counsellor would – apart from students themselves – be potential employers, professional bodies, accreditation and registration committees, other course selectors and potential clients. On the basis of Rowntree's two key functions, it is possible to infer two types of assessment. These are usually described as formative and summative (Gibbs,

1990; Rowntree, 1981). Formative assessment provides information that helps to monitor students' progress. It is obtained *during* the course, solely for the purpose of feedback to the students and staff. It may contribute to students' self-appraisal and may be used by staff to improve their teaching. Summative assessment provides information on the final level of student achievement in each completed unit or at the *end* of the course. The outcome of summative assessment will determine whether the student proceeds to the next stage or year of the course or receives the final award on completing the whole course.

Course staff with an assessment role may be only too familiar with the potential for confusion and conflict between formative and summative assessment. For instance, with formative assessment or informal feedback, students may see their trainer as a tutor, guide and friend, yet with summative assessment trainers may be seen as judge or inquisitor. Thus, students may be reluctant to reveal knowledge of their difficulties that would enable the trainer to help them, because they fear it may ultimately count against them in any final assessment. Throughout the course students tend to experience staff as supportive and on their side and then at the end of the course see staff as the final arbiters of their success. While the potential conflict can be sensitively managed, 'it never goes away entirely and is responsible for much of the mixed feelings both staff and students have about assessment' (Rowntree, 1981, p. 180).

## FORMATIVE ASSESSMENT

In most counsellor training courses formative assessment or informal feedback is given by staff or by students to each other, both written and orally, in a variety of situations: structured skills training, counselling practicum groups, supervision, personal and professional development groups. In addition feedback is given on draft written assignments and on journals or professional logs that students may keep throughout the course. Feedback is vital to learning. Students need to know their strengths or what they have done well and their relative weaknesses or what aspects they need to develop, but they need this information promptly. A few weeks on and they may be working on the next assignment and have neither time or interest to pay close attention to any feedback. Nevertheless, students will remain sensitive to feedback and counsellor trainers are often skilled at balancing negative and positive comments and turning criticisms into suggestions for ways to undertake the next piece of work.

Peer feedback or assessment is an important aspect of many counsellor training courses, yet trainers often assume that students have the knowledge and skills to give and receive feedback effectively. We advocate that the principles and practice of feedback are included in the course curriculum. A useful source is Hopson and Scally (1981). While we recognize the enormous value and potency of formative assessment in counsellor training, in this chapter we focus on summative assessment.

## SUMMATIVE ASSESSMENT

It is essential that a summary of the assessment scheme is published in the course leaflet and publicity material. At the very beginning of the course students should receive written details of all the assessment requirements. These should provide answers to two key questions: What will be assessed? and, How will it be assessed? We will deal with each of these questions in turn.

## WHAT TO ASSESS

If the assessment scheme is to be educationally valid, it should be explicitly related to the purpose and objectives of the course. Taken together, the summative assessment items should enable students to demonstrate the knowledge, skills and attitudes – or feelings, values and commitments that have been acquired or improved upon during the course. What is to be assessed will be determined by the actual content of the curriculum. The criteria for assessment need to include not only knowledge and comprehension, but equally, the cognitive skills that involve higher-order intellectual processes, such as analysis, interpretation, synthesis and evaluation (Bloom, 1975). These higher-level processes or abilities somehow transform the remembered and go beyond it (Rowntree, 1981). Nevertheless, it is a fallacy to believe that knowing how to do something is an adequate basis on which to assess the ability to actually do it. For example, a good case study may demonstrate the knowledge of how to counsel and the ability to reflect on practice, but will not necessarily demonstrate the level of skill achieved in doing so.

In practice, the distinction between knowledge and skills is not always clear-cut. In relegating this issue to a matter of academic interest we can avoid getting into a polemic debate; however, we regard it as absolutely essential that professional counsellor training courses attempt to assess practical counselling skills. Skills are concerned with the application of theory, and may be defined as 'identifiable units of goal-directed behaviour' (Hargie et al., 1981). In this sense a skill is a particular response or intervention made by a counsellor with a specific purpose or intention in mind. Such skills might include a reflection of feelings, a paraphrase of meaning, a summary, the use of open, probe and hypothetical questions and so on. We believe that it is possible to identify a range of skills applicable within any theoretical orientation. Jacobs (1988) takes a similar view. Counselling skills are usually inter-related. So, for example, 'active listening' is a multiple skill comprising smaller behavioural units such as giving full attention, observing client non-verbal behaviours, using minimal prompts – eye contact and nods – and communicating empathy with a paraphrase or reflection. Courses often produce a checklist of skills to be demonstrated – sometimes incorporating a scale on which to indicate the quality of a skill or the frequency at which it was used in an appropriate situation. Elsewhere in this book we have emphasized the need for counsellors-in-training to develop the ability to reflect on their practice. The assessment of skills should include awareness of intention, that is, what the counsellor was trying to achieve in using a particular intervention, and awareness of impact, or the extent to which the intention was achieved together with its affect on the client. This may be assessed using some form of oral or written commentary on actual practice.

Behavioural skill, or the ability to do something in an appropriate way in a given situation, is far more difficult to assess than knowledge or cognitive skill. Students need to be given far more time in which to achieve any assessable skills than to acquire assessable knowledge. Trainers will need to decide which skills must be assessed directly from a live demonstration or from an audio or video recording of a counselling interaction, which can be inferred from other activities such as process reports or case notes, and which skills can be taken for granted.

## Assessment of content

All key elements of the content of the course may require to be assessed. Some of the assessment items will measure the extent to which students have achieved the objectives for particular units of the course, while other items will be so dependent upon the course as a whole, that they require students to integrate learning from a number of separate units or objectives. The structure of the course will determine the structure of the assessment scheme but some form of summative assessment will necessarily be made of a student's knowledge of the core theoretical model, alternative models and other substantive elements of theory, the use of supervision and the ability to reflect on practice, practical counselling skills, and personal and professional development. Some assessment will be concerned with the standard of learning achieved, while other types of assessment will be concerned with something having been done, rather than how it has been done. For instance, the course will need to assess whether a student has completed the necessary minimum requirements for client work hours, supervision hours and the amount of personal counselling or self-development work.

## Competence to practise

The simple answer to the question 'What should be assessed?' must be a student's competence to practise as a counsellor. What is crucial is that in formulating the aims and objectives for the course, decisions need to be made about the knowledge, skills and attitudes a person requires in order to practise, safely and effectively, as a counsellor. Students are heavily influenced by the assessment scheme. They tend to study those topics and practise those skills which they think are most likely to be assessed. Gibbs and Habeshaw (1990) suggest that the assessment scheme is the most powerful tool for influencing student learning. It can be used to direct students' attention to what really matters. It is for this reason that systematic course design starts by determining targets for student learning outcomes or performance. The key question is 'What should students know, feel and be able to do at the end of the course?' The assessment scheme should be designed to elicit this kind of outcome or performance.

## HOW TO ASSESS

There are a number of sub-issues: Who will assess? The role of external examiners. What methods are used to assess? How to assess and record the level achieved? We will deal with each in turn.

## Who will assess?

The preferred assessment strategy of the course staff may have to be adapted to fit in with the general assessment policy of the institution or the external validating body. In BAC-recognized courses, the mode of assessment and, by implication, who will assess, should be congruent with the philosophy and rationale of the core theoretical model. So for example, a Person-Centred course would inevitably have some form of self-assessment and a formal oral or written examination assessed by staff would not be consistent with the core theoretical model.

In considering who will assess, a course needs to decide not only who carries out the assessment of each assignment, but, also, who decides the elements of the curriculum to which the assessment will relate, who decides precisely what students are to be asked to do for assessment purposes and who acts on the results of the assessment. The published assessment scheme will need to make answers to these questions explicit. Counselling courses may involve staff, self- and peer assessment or, more typically, some combination of all three. In courses which involve staff and peer assessment of the same assignment, prior decisions have to be made about what priority is given to each and who or what procedure is to be followed to arrive at the final decision in the case of a difference of opinion or judgement.

Similarly, it is important to be clear about the locus of decision-making power where self-assessment is involved. For example, there is a world of difference between courses A and B as illustrated below.

**Course A** operates a system of self-assessment where, presuming completion of all assignments, counselling practice and supervision, the student comes to a decision on whether his or her development is sufficiently advanced to receive the diploma at this time. The course staff have the power to *mediate* this decision.

**Course B** operates the same system, except for the fact that the course staff have the power to *pose their alternative view*, but do *not* have the power to change the self-assessment decision of the student.

Although these schemes appear similar, there is in fact a huge difference in terms of the attribution of responsibility to the student or the course staff.

Even on courses in which staff assess all the students' work it is helpful to encourage students to judge their own performance. Sometimes students overlook obvious errors or submit work without thinking about what is good or bad about it or how it could be improved. The quality of students' work and their ability to judge it can be improved by requiring students to assess their own work before they submit it – for example, by asking students to write down two ways in which their work is good, and two ways in which it might be improved.

## The role of external examiners

The issues concerning the appointment and role of external examiners were discussed in the chapter on staffing and resources. Here we will describe the duties and function of the external examiner. The precise nature of the duties will vary within the regulations of each institution, but will typically involve similar functions to those we outline below.

1. While external examiners will normally not be expected to become involved in the actual marking of students' work, they may be asked

to approve the procedures and content of the assessment scheme.
2. External examiners receive a previously agreed number and representative sample of each of the written assessment items. The sample would include any borderline pass/fail and pass/distinction or equivalent borderline categories. The external would moderate the standard and consistency of the internal marking. Most externals would expect to receive a copy of the guidelines and criteria given to students, together with a copy of the staff feedback given to each student in the sample and a complete mark list for the particular cohort of students.
3. The external examiner may need to visit the course to observe any form of practical work assessment.
4. Some counselling courses require an oral examination as part of the formal assessment procedure, but even where it is not a formal requirement, some institutions recognize that the external examiner has the right to conduct a viva voce examination if he or she so wishes. However, it is normal for this to be used only to confirm or improve a candidate's marks.
5. The external examiner may be involved in discussions relating to any student who may be required to withdraw from the course because of unsatisfactory progress or failure to achieve the required standard of work or who displays conduct that is considered to be unethical or unprofessional.
6. The external examiner is usually consulted about any proposed changes to the assessment scheme.

The only other people who are normally involved in the assessment process are the members of the examination or assessment board. The membership of such a board normally consists of the central staff team, the external examiner(s) and a chairperson – someone in senior management who is not directly involved in the course. In universities the chairperson would usually be the head of the department in which the course is based. Assessment boards normally meet once a year. They are concerned to ensure that the published assessment procedures have been followed and to ratify the assessment results. The decision to make the final award or to permit students to continue into the next year or stage of the course will be made by the board.

## What methods are used to assess?

There are many ways of getting to know about a student's knowledge, skills and attitudes. Most assessment methods belong either wholly or partially to one or other of two broad types:

1. Written products – like essays, journals, case studies, reports, log recording, self-appraisals, projects and transcripts of a counselling session with a written commentary.
2. Activities – like a seminar presentation, small group discussion, oral viva, demonstration of counselling skills, structured simulation, client work and personal counselling hours.

An effective assessment scheme will use a variety of these methods of assessment.

The conventional three-hour written examination in which students write answers to a specified number of previously unseen questions without access to books or other sources is a poor way to assess students, especially on counsellor training courses. Gibbs and Habeshaw (1990) suggest that examinations require a type of performance that puts a premium on memory, conformity, competition and speed and that it is unlike anything else students will have to do in life. Examinations cannot be used to predict subsequent performance as a counsellor. Most counsellor training courses do not use formal written examinations.

The method chosen to assess a particular aspect or unit of the course will be determined by the learning objective. So, for instance, if the objective is to present an argument, an analysis or evaluation, or a review of what is thought to be the relevant facts and some conclusion about them, then an essay would be the most suitable method. If the objective is concerned with how a student actually works with a client, then there may be no valid substitute for observing it being done, either live or by using an audio or video tape-recording. The issue is one of validity. That is, is the chosen method the best way to give an accurate picture of the knowledge, skills or attitudes that are to be examined?

Another decision that has to be made when considering methods of assessment is how far the course wants to control what the students do. There is a continuum between what Rowntree (1981) refers to as controlled and open assessment methods. At the controlled end would be the conventional unseen examination or the set essay question. At the other extreme, the students would be free to design their own assessment methods either individually or as a course group. Most counselling courses select methods of assessment, mid-way along this continuum: methods which require students to complete written work in their own time and at their own speed but handing it in by a given deadline. The issue of controlled or open assessment methods will be influenced by the core theoretical model, with, for example, Person-Centred courses being likely to select more open methods. In our experience it is useful for students at least to be involved in, even if not taking responsibility for, the generation of criteria against which some pieces of work will be assessed. This is especially germane for practical work.

## How to assess and record the level achieved

The assessment of essays, reports and practical skills can be a highly subjective activity. A key issue is that of reliability. It is very difficult to ensure that different assessors would give the same mark to a piece of writing or to the process skills they have observed or even whether the same assessor would give the same mark to the same piece of work, but on a different occasion. One way of increasing reliability is to make the nature of the assessment task as clear as possible for students. This can be done by providing written guidelines making explicit what they are being asked to do, what they should concentrate upon and what they should not overemphasize. The orientation of students is helped if they are shown an example of an acceptable outcome or good piece of work. If written work is required to be typed, with sub-headings, with specific sections in a particular order and of a certain length and with a particular form of annotation or referencing, then students can be shown examples of similar products. Perhaps the most important way of increasing reliability is to produce an explicit set of criteria and how the criteria will be used in allocating marks. The criteria have to describe exactly what a student needs to do in order to satisfy the required standard to pass or achieve certain grades or levels of achievement. All assessors involved in the same assessment item need to agree and have a thorough working knowledge of the criteria as well as having explicit instructions on how to apply them. Another way to establish standards and reliability is to second-mark pieces of work. This may take an inordinate amount of staff time, but can be carried out for at least one or two sample items to check standards among different assessors. It is also important to second-mark any borderline work, for example, pass/fail or pass/distinction.

We do not like the use of percentages. A percentage mark implies what we believe is an entirely spurious precision or accuracy of discriminating between levels of achievement. We do not think it is possible or necessarily desirable to determine the differences between say 61 per cent and 65 per cent. Awarding percentages, or even A–E grades, encourages competition between students and what we believe is an unnecessary and odious comparison of the abilities of one individual in relation to others. We prefer a simple pass/fail system which basically emphasizes the need for counsellor training courses to assess at the level of 'competence to practise'. However, some institutions may require grades, percentages, or a 'distinction' category, all of which beg questions of reliability in the minds of students.

The indicative standard or level of achievement will tend to reflect the type of course and nature of the final award, whether it is a certificate, diploma, first degree or postgraduate or Masters degree award. However, institutions tend to define these awards in different ways and so a particular award will not necessarily represent anything other than a very broadly based equivalent professional or academic qualification. Some courses do not have any final award on successful completion of the course. This does not matter, providing competence to practise as a counsellor is adequately assessed. There is a current trend in education towards 'profiling'. A profile provides a description of individual qualities and identifies the skills or competencies achieved and could be used to complement, or even replace, a final award.

The whole issue of assessment is complicated and fraught with difficulties. A lucid account of the issues and methods of assessment is provided by Rowntree (1987). Gibbs and Habeshaw (1990) provide another useful source.

## ASSESSMENT SCHEME CONTENTS

We have already said how important it is that students receive a copy of the assessment scheme at the very start of the course. The scheme should contain the regulations and procedures for the final award or successful completion of the course. Each assignment or item of assessment should be clearly identified. The description of each item needs to include the indicative content or what is being assessed, the criteria for assessment, how the item will be assessed and by whom, some indication of the length or the number of words required for any written element and the date of submission. The satisfactory completion of the required number of client work hours and – if required – personal counselling hours would be included as items of assessment.

The assessment scheme should explain the marking system, e.g. percentages, A–E grades, or pass/fail categories. It should also explain how many items are required and at what level in order to proceed to the next year or stage of the course.

In addition the scheme should explain the procedure and regulations for referred and deferred work. Referred work is that which fails to reach the required minimum standard and has to be re-submitted, usually within a specified time. The regulations for some courses only permit the re-submission of one or two items, while other courses accept the re-submission of all or most items and are prepared to condone the failure of one or more items at the discretion of the assessment board. Deferred work is work that has not actually been submitted by the student. The assessment regulations need to explain the procedure for the late submission of work and any penalties that may accrue. For example, it may not be possible to gain a distinction on deferred work or written feedback may not be given. It is usual to require that referred and deferred work is to be satisfactorily completed before students are permitted to continue into the next year or stage of the course. In recent years, courses are beginning to pay attention to the need to assess a student's readiness before allowing them to start work with clients (see Chapter 9). However, this means that some students may have to defer a specified number of the required minimum number of client work hours until after the completion of the course, but before the final award is made. This is now fairly common practice and helps to safeguard the interests of clients by avoiding the totally unethical situation in which students start working with clients before they are capable of doing so, while at the same time ensuring that students gain sufficient client work experience before completing the course. Students who defer what must be a specified and limited amount of client work only, would be expected to submit a client work log, case notes and evidence of adequate supervision.

The assessment scheme might also describe the membership and role of the assessment board, when the board is held and the procedures for students to follow if they want the board to consider any 'mitigating circumstances' that might be taken into account in the event that the student may otherwise fail the course or a particular piece of work or be on the borderline of a higher level of award. The assessment scheme might include a summary of the duties of the external examiner and contain some reference to an appeals procedure.

## APPEALS PROCEDURE

Universities and colleges will normally have a published appeals procedure for all courses run by the institution. Other organizations that run counsellor training courses may have to develop a procedure specifically for the course. If a student wants to dispute a decision of the assessment board, it would normally be possible for a student to appeal in accordance with the assessment regulations. Appeals may normally be against a decision or recommendation that: the student has failed the course or part of the course, the student should not be permitted to proceed to the next stage of the course, or that the student should be excluded from continuing to study on the course. An appeal is normally admissible on the grounds that the assessment procedures failed to accord with the assessment scheme regulations, or that the board failed to take proper account of any mitigating circumstances. In most institutions the appeals regulations state that appeals cannot be entertained on matters of academic judgement. Academic judgements are concerned with such decisions as whether a student has reached the required academic standard required by the course or whether the student would benefit from further study. Appeals regulations typically require students to lodge notice of their intention to appeal, to a specified person other than a member of the central staff team, within a specified period after the publication of the results.

Fortunately, appeals are infrequent, but nevertheless a course must have an explicit and published procedure, adequate to deal with such situations, when and if they occur.

## ACCREDITATION OF PRIOR LEARNING (APL)

APL is now a familiar concept in education and training, but as yet has had relatively little impact on counsellor training. The British Association for Counselling is currently working on developing ways in which APL might be introduced into the BAC courses recognition scheme.

The accreditation or assessment of prior learning is essentially a process that enables people to receive formal recognition for the skills and knowledge they already possess. The type of recognition varies, but could be in the form of credit towards a particular qualification or exemption from some portion of a training programme. Simosko (1991, p. 12) suggests that APL is about four basic processes:

identifying what an individual can do or knows;

equating those skills and knowledge with specific standards, course or qualification requirements;

assessing the individual against those standards or requirements;

crediting the learner in whatever way is appropriate.

In applying for APL, people normally prepare a portfolio that demonstrates their competence and provides evidence to substantiate their claim to credit. The primary task is to make sure that the portfolio contains sufficient and valid evidence to prove that applicants really know and can do what they claim. APL has considerable resource implications for the course, both in terms of staff time and further training. Preparing a portfolio is a complicated process and courses need to provide elaborate instructions, extensive guidelines as well as training workshops for applicants, in order to help them to construct their portfolios. Many people find APL a much more demanding process than they initially anticipated. Done properly, APL is far from being a soft option that threatens to reduce standards. For courses interested in exploring the possibility of offering some form of assessment of prior learning, we recommend two excellent source books by Simosko (1991, 1992).

This chapter has examined the issues related to the assessment of students coursework; in the final chapter we look at the issues related to the evaluation of the course.

# THIRTEEN
# Evaluation

One of the key issues in education and training in the 1990s is 'quality assurance'. This is concerned with the evaluation or appraisal of the quality of the course. The link between evaluation and accountability is very strong. In an expanding and competitive market, counsellor training courses have become increasingly accountable both to the consumers or students and to the employers or the institution in which the course is based, as well as to external academic or professional bodies that may validate the course. What happens in courses is no longer a matter of concern only for staff. Staff do not have the same degree of personal autonomy that they had a decade or so ago – their work is increasingly coming under public scrutiny.

Worthwhile evaluation takes time and resources. It is not something that can be tackled on the last day of the course or as an afterthought when the course has ended. An effective evaluation system needs to be planned as an integral part of the delivery of counsellor training.

Being the subject of evaluation is not easy. For many staff, the very idea of their work being evaluated induces a defensive reaction. Staff can feel vulnerable to potential criticism and threatened by the prospect of negative judgements being made about them and their work. It is sometimes hard for people who invest so much of themselves in what they do and for whom their work role is a major source of identity, to separate evaluation of their work from evaluation of themselves as people. Counsellors will be only too familiar with this phenomenon in their work with clients. It is important that evaluation is not seen as an opportunity for the 'consumer to strike back', but rather as an on-going dialogue and collaborative venture. If staff can model genuine openness, avoiding signs of approval or disapproval in response to positive or negative feedback, then students may be helped to do the same. Evaluation can be a collaborative venture when both staff and students take joint responsibility for the outcomes. Thus evaluation can become a creative source of learning that informs both students and staff about their respective contribution to the course. Evaluation works best if students themselves feel that they are not mere 'consumers' but participants in, and contributors to, an evolving process of learning.

In this chapter we will discuss the issues relating to the following questions: Why evaluate? Who is involved in evaluation? What should be evaluated? How should evaluation be done? and How should evaluation information be used? In the final section of this chapter we will look at complaints procedures and the issues related to codes of ethics and practice.

## WHY EVALUATE?

The ultimate goal of course evaluation is to improve the quality of the course. However, evaluation is carried out for a variety of reasons. A cynical or political reason, yet nonetheless germane in the present climate, is to prove that it has been done. The main purpose of evaluation is to understand what has been going on, so as to be able to make informed decisions about the course. Managers and administrators will want to know whether there is sufficient demand for the course and whether the cost of mounting it is justified. They will want an annual audit of these and other market research and budgeting issues. Professional bodies, such as the British Association for Counselling or universities that validate courses in other institutions, will want to know whether the course has attained or is maintaining the required standards. Courses seek external academic validation or professional recognition to improve their status and credibility. External validation or recognition is seen as likely to enhance marketability and help to ensure the course's survival. Institutions and the staff that run the course will be concerned with how to sustain, develop and improve it. The students themselves will want to know whether the course continues to satisfy any external validation, such as BAC recognition, as this may affect the status of their final award. Students will also want to feel that they have ample opportunity to comment on their experience of the course and influence how it is run. An advantage of placing evaluation at various stages throughout the course is that improvements resulting from the feedback may be implemented immediately, thus benefiting current as well as future students. Course evaluation is also useful for potential applicants who will be interested in what the course is like, the drop-out rates, workloads and other costs (financial or otherwise) that might be involved in taking the course. They will be interested in whether the course is validated by BAC or some other professional body and take this as an assurance of the quality of training and the relevance of the final award to their subsequent professional development.

## WHO IS INVOLVED IN EVALUATION?

Evaluation was originally seen as a task for external bodies, such as HMI (Her Majesty's Inspectorate), now replaced in England and Wales by OFSTED (Office for Standards in Education) and Local Education Authorities, although private counsellor training organizations have hitherto been largely immune from such forms of external evaluation. What seems to have happened in the last decade is a shift towards institution- or organization-initiated evaluation. Clements and Pearce (1986) see this development as a reflection of the change in the ways data are collected for research and evaluation. They suggest that the traditional popularity of 'objective' methodologies gave way to more subjective, illuminative or qualitative approaches. The greater emphasis on internal evaluation also reflects the increasing autonomy of institutions within the education system and the fact that they have had to assume responsibility for demonstrating their accountability to the outside world.

Universities, colleges and similar institutions usually have some form of academic standards committee to validate a course before it can run. Once a course has started it is then subject to annual audits and reports from external examiners, as well as to more extensive triennial reviews and major re-validation events every five or six years. Membership of internal academic standards or quality assurance committees is typically drawn from senior management, professional and academic staff outside the department in which the course is run, together with several external 'experts'. Private training organizations usually have training or management committees with a similar remit and with similar procedures for course evaluation.

Evaluation invariably requires a contribution from people outside the course or organization. BAC-recognized courses would expect to involve three such external people, whose roles were discussed in Chapter 6 on staffing and resources: the external examiner, the course consultant and the complaints mediator.

Ultimately the people who are inescapably bound up in the whole process of evaluation are the course staff and students. Students are the principal source of evaluative data and the central staff team remain the principal agents of the process, responsible for gathering, analysing and presenting the results of evaluation.

## WHAT SHOULD BE EVALUATED?

We will outline the issues for evaluation at different stages of the course operation. We will look at ongoing evaluation and the annual audit, evaluation of specific parts of the course and self-evaluation.

### On-going evaluation: the annual audit

On-going evaluation, for example the annual audit or review, will be especially concerned with what problems or issues have emerged and what changes and improvements have been made to each of the key elements of the training. In discussing evaluation Rowntree (1981) distinguishes between 'effects' and 'effectiveness'. He argues that 'effectiveness' or goal-based evaluation implies concern with the extent to which the course has been successful in achieving certain pre-specified ends or goals. While this is important, evaluation should also be concerned with course 'effects' or 'goal-free' outcomes that were not anticipated. If evaluation is to be worthwhile, Rowntree argues that we cannot afford to overlook the unexpected or unplanned.

The annual course audit will typically involve gathering the following data:

- number of applications received, the number of applicants interviewed, the number of offers of places made and how many were accepted
- number of students in each cohort or year group, how many proceeded to the next stage or year of the course, how many dropped out and their reasons for doing so
- number of students who passed the course and at what level
- destination information about employment after the course or how students used their qualification
- student feedback and evaluation, including a summary of the most positive aspects, and the major problems or criticisms
- the external examiner's evaluation
- how staff responded to any critical feedback from students or the external examiner and any changes or solutions to problems or issues that emerged during the year
- proposed developments or improvements to the course content, structure or methods together with the rationale or justification for any proposed changes
- staff professional and academic development activities
- achievements or outstanding aspects of the course
- issues outside the responsibility of the staff team, such as problems with institutional administration, accommodation, resources and facilities.

The annual course report is an opportunity for staff to emphasize the need for their own continuing clinical work and supervision as an integral part of their work as trainers. Institutions still tend to be reluctant to credit staff with time for clinical work and tend to regard empirical research and giving conference papers as the only valid form of professional or academic development. Yet the external validity of a course may be threatened if staff fail to maintain their own clinical practice.

## Evaluating specific parts of the course

The key questions to ask participants when evaluating a session or workshop are:

- What did you like most about the session?
- What did you dislike most about it?
- What changes would you like to see made?

In evaluating a series of workshops or a course unit, more thorough evaluation might include such issues as:

- Were the aims and objectives made sufficiently clear?
- Was the content appropriately challenging without being inaccessible?
- Were the students helped to acquire factual knowledge, learn and apply principles and concepts, develop practical skills, and/or enhance self-reflection and self-understanding?
- Was the structure coherent, with an appropriate balance of practical work and theoretical input, with adequate demonstrations and illustrative case material and with opportunities for discussion and reflection or feedback?
- Were the sessions carefully planned and flexible enough to adapt to the needs and interests of students?
- Was the style of presentation lively and engaging, with appropriate ways of stimulating interest?
- Was adequate concern shown for how individuals coped with the demands of the work?
- Were the handouts useful and clearly presented?
- Were the teaching methods and the range and depth of material likely to enable students to achieve the intended outcomes?
- Was the assessment directly relevant to the aims and objectives and clear in what it demanded of students?

Most of these issues explore the effectiveness of the sessions in terms of intended outcomes. Sometimes the most illuminating data can emerge from responses to an open invitation to comment on any other aspect of the students' experience. This can help to get at the often unintended ways in which the sessions were most memorable (or otherwise) in the eyes of students. General comments often convey salutary messages about how students' views differ from our own.

## Trainer self-evaluation

Most staff will be aware of their strengths and weaknesses as counsellor trainers, yet it is not always easy to look objectively at our performance in face-to-face work with students. Evaluating some of our own teaching sessions can help to gain a better understanding of ourselves. One way to do this is to use a checklist or, better still, an audiotape recording of it to review our impression of a session.

This self-evaluation checklist is adapted from Rowntree (1981, p. 281).

Was the accommodation suitable (e.g. arrangement of seats, etc.)?
Was the session carefully planned?
Did the plan prove appropriate?
Were the objectives clear to the students?
Was the content well structured?
Was the time available adequate to cover all aspects?
Were the methods and media appropriate?
Were the methods and media used successfully?
Was the 'social climate' conducive to learning?
Did students participate appropriately?
Am I satisfied with what was learned?
Do I think the students were satisfied with what they gained
from the session? How do I know?
What would I do differently another time?

We are not suggesting that it is necessary or even desirable to evaluate every session but to select certain critical sessions to evaluate, e.g. those that were new or felt difficult in some way or another.

The recently revised BAC Code of Ethics and Practice for Trainers (1995, A2.3) states that counsellor trainers should 'regularly monitor and evaluate the limits of their competence as trainers by means of regular supervision or consultancy'.

It is possible to argue that supervision or consultancy excludes a colleague on the grounds of objectivity, yet reciprocal peer supervision and evaluation offers a practical and valid alternative to employing an outside supervisor or consultant. What we advocate is that all staff trainers should discuss their work not less than once every two or three months. This would be a comparable process to the supervision of client work, but with trainers presenting their work with students. An alternative is for the supervision of the work of trainers to be done within the staff team. This might enable the staff group as a whole to allow individual members maximum opportunity to use their strengths and compensate for their weaknesses with the co-operation of others who have more knowledge or experience in complementary areas. However, even with a clear contract, but without an external facilitator, there is always the risk of collusion. This underlines the importance of regular staff meetings with the course consultant, who can create the conditions where hitherto unspoken tensions may be raised and considered openly.

## HOW TO EVALUATE?

There are several dimensions on which evaluation procedures may vary:

internal–external
formative–summative
formal–informal

We have already discussed the need for both internal evaluation initiated by the course or institution and external evaluation conducted by external bodies. The formative and summative dimension relates to the purpose of evaluation. Sometimes information about the success of the course or a particular unit is sought by staff solely for the purpose of revising and improving it. This kind of evaluation is usually called 'formative', because it contributes to the forming or shaping of the existing course (Barnes, 1982). The purpose of summative evaluation is to consider the course as a whole and to decide whether or not it deserves continuing support by the institution. Summative evaluation can be used to improve subsequent versions of the course.

Most staff trainers will pause for a moment to reflect on how their last training session went. They will have at least some sense of whether it went well or not. This judgement is likely to be based on several things, for instance, whether there was falling class attendance, how attentive and interested the students appeared to be, the extent to which students seem to understand and make appropriate contributions and the quality of any written or practical work done. Sometimes the changes staff make to their teaching style, content of the session or methods used are based on evidence no more substantial than this. At times the evidence used to make informal evaluations of a session may be too impressionistic and derived from very limited sources. It is very easy to overreact and even plan changes on the opinion of one disgruntled student, or feel good about a session because one or two students made a point of saying how much they had enjoyed it. We are not suggesting that staff ignore informal evaluation that arises naturally and spontaneously from discussion about 'how things are going' during individual tutorials, course group meetings, coffee breaks and similar occasions. Staff should encourage and remain open to casual feedback from students. They need to be alert to signs that things are going adrift, or that good things may have happened. Such feedback contributes to the informal monitoring of the course. However, it is also important to incorporate, within the timetabled course programme, formal and systematic procedures for gathering data on which to evaluate the course.

Formal evaluation differs from informal evaluation in that it actively seeks to obtain specific kinds of information. Rather than simply being on the look-out for anything that might indicate how the course is going, answers to certain questions are deliberately sought using a whole variety of methods of data collection.

*Structured reviews.* A checklist of issues or questions can provide a useful agenda for a formal evaluation session. Individual students may be invited to reflect for a few minutes on their experience, then join together in pairs or in a small group to share ideas and prepare written feedback to be given to staff. Alternatively, individual students could write down three statements about the course or unit, which, with successive pooling as the groups combine, are written on flip chart paper and given a rating in turn by everyone. A useful plenary discussion may follow.

*Checklists.* These can be used as a form of questionnaire in which students are asked to indicate the extent of their agreement or disagreement with a series of statements. An example of a statement might be 'The aims and objectives were made clear'. Students might respond with either 'yes' or 'no' or rate their reaction to the statement on a continuum. Alternatively, a numerical five-point scale from 1 to 5, with 5 indicating a very high level of agreement, could be used.

*Observation.* Observation occupies a central place in most approaches to evaluation. Observing staff and students at work can be undertaken as a participant or non-participant. Clements and Pearce (1986, p. 85) suggest that 'there is little doubt that participant observation can offer unrivalled insights' and argue that the only people qualified to describe adequately what is going on within a session are the participants. There are disadvantages with any form of evaluation by observers. The very presence of an observer, even if participating in the work being observed, can still feel like an intrusion and may change the situation by influencing participants' behaviour. Some trainers co-teach with a colleague, who for some of the time acts as a participant observer. As these staff colleagues will be known to the students they may be experienced as less of an intrusion.

*Questionnaires.* Questionnaires can be the most effective method of collecting information. They can be used to elicit a great number of responses from every participant. There are disadvantages in that some recipients regard questionnaires as impersonal or find their limitations frustrating. Anonymous questionnaires can encourage frank responses, but there are often problems of misinterpretation – both of the questions and of the answers – and these cannot be followed up. However, if used in conjunction with other methods, questionnaires can substantiate or qualify other findings and back up impressions gained from casual or informal evaluation. Questionnaires can utilize various types of questions, including: unfinished sentences, closed questions, open questions, multiple-choice questions, checklists and rating a given set of statements. A valuable reference on the design and use of questionnaires is Youngman (1987). The considerable time needed to prepare the questionnaire and analyse the results is unavoidable, so elaborate questionnaires will probably be used only for end of course evaluation or at the end of some discrete and important unit of the course.

## HOW SHOULD EVALUATION INFORMATION BE USED?

In the beginning of this chapter we explained the reasons for evaluating a course and how the information is needed to demonstrate accountability. We also discussed why evaluation is required by the organization that runs the course and how it is used as an integral part of any external recognition or validation of the course.

We regard the ultimate purpose of evaluation as a way of getting to know what is really going on in the course so as to sustain it, develop it and, where possible, improve it.

Rowntree (1987) suggests that evaluation can enable staff to develop and improve:

- the existing course for the current students
- future versions of the same course for subsequent students
- future courses for perhaps quite different students.

Courses may want to keep a written record of evaluation outcomes. This can be used for the annual course report and other requests made to the course to account for what is going on. Having collected and analysed the evaluation data, the implications for action need to be considered by the central staff team and may be discussed with students. Some courses give students a copy of the summarized evaluation responses to questionnaires and other methods of data collection. Discussion between staff and students of the evaluation findings can be a valuable learning device. It can sometimes reveal issues that the questionnaires or other methods glossed over or did not touch upon at all. It can also help to clarify misunderstanding. One of the biggest difficulties in responding to evaluation by making changes to the course is that evaluation data typically contain ambiguous and often contradictory opinions and views. It is easy to be over-impressed by certain comments because they happen to have been given in a particularly vociferous way and often without evidence that the comments represent anything but a minority view. It seems important that changes to the course result from a consensus view and from information obtained from a variety of sources and by a variety of methods. Yet another risk in responding to evaluation data lies in being so overwhelmed by the sheer volume of diverse information that one sees only the feedback that confirms what the staff want to do to the course anyway. This can be guarded against, to some extent, by involving an external consultant to facilitate staff course review meetings. Discussing course evaluation data among the staff team can help to get negative and very critical evaluation into perspective – especially for staff who may be discouraged because they feel they should be pleasing all the students all the time. (Pleasing most of the students some of the time is a more realistic aspiration!)

At least twice a year, but preferably every three months or so, staff meetings may be designated for discussing course evaluation and whether it is possible and desirable to introduce any changes to the current course. It is important to respond to evaluation, but Rowntree (1981) warns of the danger of trying to respond too fast or too drastically. Big changes are best phased in gradually, being careful not to lose aspects that work well in haste to improve those that do not. Any innovation or different way of working will have its own teething troubles and doubtless bring its own problems. Each year has different students and their needs and interests will be different from previous cohorts. These and other factors will interact to make the course a different experience each time it runs. Continuous monitoring, evaluation with the introduction of changes and improvements will never achieve the 'perfect course'. Evaluation is an integral part of the process of running a course.

## FEEDBACK AND COMPLAINTS

BAC-recognized courses are required to publish appeals and complaints procedures. In Chapter 12 on assessment we looked at the issues concerned with students appealing against their assessment results or against decisions that they have failed the course or that they have to re-take a year or stage of the course. We will now look at formal complaints made about the institution, the course or the professional or ethical conduct of staff.

Counsellor training courses will normally provide many opportunities for students to give feedback and evaluation. Course 'community meetings', casual feedback and formal review and evaluation sessions are all opportunities for students to express their concerns or misgivings about what has been happening in the course. Alternatively, students can raise any problems or complaints about the course with their personal tutor, the course tutor or any other appropriate member of staff. Who to see for what purpose can be explained in the evaluation procedures published in the course handbook.

## A COMPLAINTS PROCEDURE

A complaints procedure is designed to offer an independent hearing of complaints by students or by members of the public who have contact with or some information about the course. The course will need to appoint an external mediator to receive complaints. It is likely that such a person will have some knowledge of the course, but it is important that the mediator has no previous or current links with the organization nor any previous or current professional or social relationship with any member of staff. The external mediator needs to be seen clearly as independent and unbiased.

A complainant should invoke the complaints procedure only after all internal procedures and negotiations are complete and the complainant is not satisfied with the outcomes.

Most complaints procedures will have similar guidelines to the following:

1. The complainant puts her or his case in writing and sends it to the external mediator.

2. On receipt of the complaint the mediator informs the course of the nature of the complaint.

3. Within a specified period, normally 14 days, the course staff will send a written report to the mediator, explaining their view of what has happened and the action that has been taken.

4. There may then follow a limited period of written communication between the mediator and the people concerned in order to clarify

aspects of the documentation. The length of this period should be specified in the Complaints Procedure and would normally be not more than 28 days.

5. On the basis of the information received, the mediator will inform the course and the complainant of her or his recommendations. It is normal not to require mediators to give reasons or justify their recommendations.

6. The mediator may wish to meet the complainant and also decide that it is appropriate to arrange a separate meeting with a representative of the course. It is expected that such meetings would only take place on the matter of serious ethical complaints.

7. In special circumstances the mediator may recommend a meeting between the complainant and a representative of the course. The mediator would normally facilitate such a meeting in which the complainant may be accompanied by a 'friend'.

8. The course would normally agree to act on the recommendations of the mediator, but any likely conditions or constraints on the course to implement recommendations should be stated in the complaints procedure. For example, courses may also be bound by their own institution's appeals and complaints procedures.

9. The published complaints procedure should contain the name and address of the mediator or otherwise explain how the mediator can be contacted.

10. The complaints procedure should indicate who is responsible for paying the mediator's fee and expenses. This is paid preferably by the organization or institution rather than the course.

BAC-recognized courses are required to enter into a consultative partnership with another recognized course throughout the period of recognition (BAC, 1990). Some recognized courses set up a reciprocal arrangement by which each course provides a named mediator for the other.

Participating in the course's own complaints procedure does not preclude other action by the complainant. The most obvious example is that, regardless of the recommendations of the mediator and providing the course is an organizational member of BAC, the complainant may wish to invoke the BAC Complaints Procedure (BAC, 1992).

## CODES OF ETHICS AND PRACTICE

Most professional organizations have produced a code of ethics and practice. Bond (1993, p. 12) sees this as 'not only part of the emerging identity and ideology of the counsellor's role, but more pragmatically, as a way of promoting standards of practice and working towards a system of self-regulation or statutory responsibility'. The British Association for Counselling has separate and well-established codes of ethics and practice for counsellors, trainers and supervisors. These codes are subject to continued review and revision. Staff working on courses that are organizational members of BAC – including BAC-recognized courses – are required to adhere to the relevant code that covers the work they do. Such courses are subject to the BAC Complaints Procedure and are therefore ultimately responsible for ensuring that all staff, including external supervisors and sessional staff, accept and agree to work within the appropriate codes. The fact that a course is accountable to BAC in this way means that students will have some safeguards that will help to ensure professional and ethical practice and that they will also have some means of redress.

This 'accountability' factor is the essential insurance for trainees, prospective trainees and those members of the public who will be in contact with professional counselling in the future. No one can stand over counsellors throughout their life-long practice, but if their training has helped them to develop as reflective practitioners they will not only be 'accountable' to their training organization and their professional body, but also to themselves.

This brings us to the end of the book. Since we have just been considering the issue of evaluation, we invite you to evaluate our book by sending us feedback via the publishers. Thank you.

# References

Advice, Guidance and Counselling Lead Body Secretariat (AGCLB) (1994) *Consultation Standards Questionnaire*. AGCLB, 40a High Street, Welwyn, Herts AL6 9ER.

Andresen, L. (1990) Lecturing to large groups, Induction Pack I. In C. Rust (ed.), *Teaching in Higher Education*, SCED Paper 57. Birmingham Polytechnic: Standing Conference on Educational Development.

BAC (1988) *Code of Ethics and Practice for the Supervision of Counsellors*. Rugby: British Association for Counselling.

BAC (1990) *The Recognition of Counsellor Training Courses* (2nd edn). Rugby: British Association for Counselling.

BAC (1992) *Complaints Procedure*. Rugby: British Association for Counselling.

BAC (1993a) *The Recognition of Counsellor Training Courses Scheme: Guidelines for Integrative and Eclectic Courses*, BAC/CRG Information Sheet. Rugby: British Association for Counselling.

BAC (1993b) *Code of Ethics and Practice for Counsellors*. Rugby: British Association for Counselling.

BAC (1995) *Code of Ethics and Practice for Trainers*. Rugby: British Association for Counselling.

Bailey, R. D. (1985) *Coping with Stress in Caring*. Oxford: Blackwell.

Baker, S. B., Daniels, T. G. and Greeley, A. (1990) Systematic training of graduate-level counselors: narrative and meta-analytic reviews of three major programs. *Counseling Psychologist* 18, 355-421.

Barnes, D. (1982) *Practicum Curriculum Study*. London: Routledge & Kegan Paul.

Beitman, B. D. (1987) *The Structure of Individual Psychotherapy*. New York: Guilford.

Beitman, B. D. (1990) Why I am an integrationist (not an eclectic). In W. Dryden and J. C. Norcross (eds), *Eclecticism and Integration in Counselling and Psychotherapy.* Loughton, UK: Gale Centre Publications, pp. 51–70.

Beitman, B. D. (1992) Integration through fundamental similarities and useful differences among schools. In J. C. Norcross and M. R. Goldfried (eds), *Handbook of Psychotherapy Integration.* New York: Basic Books.

Bergin, A. E. and Garfield, S. L. (1994) *Handbook of Psychotherapy and Behavior Change.* New York: Wiley.

Bernard, J. M. and Goodyear, R. K. (1992) *Fundamentals of Clinical Supervision.* Boston: Allyn & Bacon.

Bimrose, J. (1993) Counselling and social context. In R. Bayne and P. Nicolson (eds), *Counselling and Psychology for Health Professionals.* London: Chapman & Hall.

Bloom, B. S. (1975) Taxonomy of educational objectives. In R. Hooper (ed.), *The Curriculum: Context, Design and Development.* Edinburgh: Oliver & Boyd in association with the Open University.

Bond, T. (1993) *Standards and Ethics for Counselling in Action.* London: Sage.

Carkhuff, R. R. (1969) *Helping and Human Relations: A Primer for Lay and Professional Helpers,* Vols 1 and 2. New York: Holt, Rinehart & Winston.

Clements, A. J. and Pearce, J. S. (1986) *The Evaluation of Pastoral Care.* Oxford: Blackwell.

CNAA (1992) The role of the course leader. Unpublished paper prepared by G. Bradley (Hull University), J. Brennan and B. Little (CNAA). London: Council for National Academic Awards.

Coate, M. A. (1994) *Guidelines for Client Work and Supervision in Recognised Courses.* Rugby: British Association for Counselling.

Deurzen-Smith, E. (1988) *Existential Counselling in Practice.* London: Sage.

Dooley, C. (1994) Professional issues in the 1990s and beyond. In S. J. E. Lindsay and G. E. Powell (eds), *Handbook of Clinical Adult Psychology.* London: Routledge, pp. 787–807.

Dryden, W. (ed.) (1992) *Integrative and Eclectic Therapy: A Handbook.* Buckingham: Open University Press.

Dryden, W. (1993) *Reflections on Counselling.* London: Whurr Publishers.

Dryden, W. (1994a) Possible future trends in counselling and counsellor training: a personal view. *Counselling* 5(3), 194–7.

Dryden, W. (1994b) *Invitation to Rational–Emotive Psychology.* London: Whurr.

Dryden, W. (ed.) (1995a) *The Stresses of Counselling in Action.* London: Sage.

Dryden, W. (1995b) *Preparing for Client Change in Rational Emotive Behaviour Therapy.* London: Whurr.

Dryden, W. and Feltham, C. (eds) (1992) *Psychotherapy and Its Discontents.* Buckingham: Open University Press.

Dryden, W. and Thorne, B. (eds) (1991) *Training and Supervision for Counselling in Action.* London: Sage.

Egan, G. (1994) *The Skilled Helper: A Systematic Approach to Effective Helping* (5th edn). Pacific Grove, CA: Brooks/Cole.

Fonagy, P. and Higgitt, A. (1984) *Personality Theory and Clinical Practice.* London: Methuen.

Ford, J.D. (1979) Research on training counselors and clinicians. *Review of Educational Research* 49, 87–130.

Gibbs, G. and Habeshaw, T. (1990). An introduction to assessment. Induction Pack IV. In C. Rust (ed.), *Teaching in Higher Education*, SCED Paper 57. Birmingham Polytechnic: Standing Conference on Educational Development.

Gibbs, G., Habeshaw, S. and Habeshaw, T. (1984) *53 Interesting Things to Do in Your Lectures.* Bristol: Technical and Educational Services.

Godden, D. (1994) Letter on training and assessment. *Counselling* 5 (4), 258.

Hansen, J. C., Stevic, R. R. and Warner, R. W. Jr (1982) *Counseling: Theory and Process* (3rd edn). Boston: Allyn & Bacon.

Hargie, O., Saunders, C. and Dickson, D. (1981) *Social Skills in Interpersonal Communication.* London: Croom Helm.

Hopson, B. and Scally, M. (1981) *Lifeskills Teaching.* London: McGraw-Hill.

Jacobs, M. (1988) *Psychodynamic Counselling in Action.* London: Sage.

Jacobs, M. (1991) *Insight and Experience: A Manual of Training in the Technique and Theory of Psychodynamic Counselling and Therapy.* Buckingham: Open University Press.

Jacobs, M. (1993) The use of audiotapes in counselling. In W. Dryden (ed.), *Questions and Answers on Counselling in Action.* London: Sage, pp. 5–9.

Johnson, D. W. and Johnson, F. P. (1975) *Joining Together: Group Theory and Group Skills.* Englewood Cliffs, NJ: Prentice Hall.

Kagan, N. (1984) Interpersonal process recall: basic methods and recent research. In D. Larson (ed.), *Teaching Psychological Skills: Models for Giving Psychology Away.* Monterey, CA: Brooks/Cole.

Kagan, N. and Kagan, M. (1990) IPR: a validated model for the 1990s and beyond. *Counseling Psychologist* 18, 436–40.

Lambert, M. J. (ed.) (1982) *Psychotherapy and Patient Relationships*. Homewood, IL: Dow Jones-Irwin.

Lebow, J. L. (1987) Developing a personal integration in family therapy: principles for model construction and practice. *Journal of Marital and Family Therapy* 13 (1), 1-14.

McMahon, G. (1993) *Setting Up Your Own Private Practice*. Cambridge, UK: NEC.

Mahrer, A. R. (1989) *The Integration of Psychotherapies*. Ottawa, Canada: Human Science Press.

Mearns, D. (1993a) Against indemnity insurance. In W. Dryden (ed.), *Questions and Answers on Counselling in Action*. London: Sage, pp. 161–4.

Mearns, D. (1993b) Diploma in Counselling (FT) Submission to BAC for Entry to the Scheme for the Recognition of Counsellor Training Courses. Glasgow: University of Strathclyde.

Mearns, D. (1994) *Developing Person-Centred Counselling*. London: Sage.

Mearns, D. and Thorne, B. (1988) *Person-Centred Counselling in Action*. London: Sage.

Menzies, I. E. P. (1970) *The Functions of Social Systems as a Defence Against Anxiety*. London: Tavistock Institute of Human Relations.

Nelson-Jones, R. (1982) *The Theory and Practice of Counselling Psychology*. Eastbourne: Holt, Rinehart & Winston.

Nelson-Jones, R. (1985) Eclecticism, integration and comprehensiveness in counselling theory and practice. *British Journal of Guidance and Counselling* 13 (2), 129–38.

Noyes, E. (1991) A survey of counselling training courses – a comparison of standards. *Counselling Psychology Review* 4 (2), 16–23.

Persaud, R. (1993) The career of counselling: careering out of control. *Journal of Mental Health* 2, 283–5.

Pfeiffer, J. W. and Jones, J. E. (1973) *A Handbook of Structured Experiences for Human Relations Training*, Vol. 4. California: University Associates.

Reber, A. S. (1985) *Dictionary of Psychology*. Harmondsworth: Penguin Books.

Rogers, C. R. (1977) Resolving intercultural tensions. In C. R. Rogers, *Carl Rogers on Personal Power*. New York: Delacorte, pp. 115–41.

Rogers, C. R. (1982) A psychologist looks at nuclear war. *Journal of Humanistic Psychology* 22 (4), 9–20.

Rowntree, D. (1981) *Developing Courses for Students*. Maidenhead: McGraw-Hill.

Rowntree, D. (1987) *Assessing Students – How Shall We Know Them?* Maidenhead: McGraw-Hill.

Samuels, A. (1993) *The Political Psyche*. London: Routledge.

Simosko, S. (1991) *Accreditation of Prior Learning: A Practical Guide for Professionals*. London: Kogan Page.

Simosko, S. (1992) *Get Qualifications for What You Know and Can Do: A Personal Guide to APL*. London: Kogan Page.

Smith, M., Glass, G. and Miller, T. (1980) *The Benefits of Psychotherapy*. Baltimore: Johns Hopkins Press.

Sue, D. W. and Sue, D. (1990) *Counseling the Culturally Different* (2nd edn). New York: Wiley.

Trower, P., Casey, A. and Dryden, W. (1988) *Cognitive-Behavioural Counselling in Action*. London: Sage.

Verba, S. (1961) *Leadership: Affective and Instrumental. In Small Groups and Political Behaviour*. Princeton, NJ: Princeton University Press.

Wallace, W. A. (1986) *Theories of Counseling and Psychotherapy: A Basic Issues Approach*. Boston: Allyn & Bacon.

Wheeler, S. (in preparation) *Assessing the Competence of Counsellors in Training*. London: Cassell.

Windt, P. Y., Appleby, P. C., Franers, L. P. and Landesman, B. M. (1991) *Ethical Issues in the Professions*. Englewood Cliffs, NJ: Prentice-Hall.

Woolfe, R. (1983) Counselling in a world of crisis: towards a sociology of counseling. *International Journal for the Advancement of Counselling* 6, 167–76.

Youngman, M. B. (1987) *Designing and Analysing Questionnaires*, Rediguide 12. Nottingham: University of Nottingham.

# Name Index

Andresen, L.   83
BAC (British Association for Counselling)
   *Code of Ethics and Practice for Counsellors*
     10, 78, 81–2, 118, 128, 130
   *Code of Ethics and Practice for the*
     *Supervision of Counsellors*   10, 44
   *Code of Ethics and Practice for Trainers*
     10, 49, 50, 150
   *Complaints Procedure*   156
   *The Recognition of Counsellor Training*
     *Courses*   2, 10, 13–14, 19, 25–6, 60,
     115, 117, 123
Bailey, R. D.   49
Baker, S. B.   95
Barnes, D.   132, 151
Beitman, B. D.   26–7, 32–3, 86
Bergin, A. E.   62, 100
Bernard, J. M.   79
Bimrose, J.   80
Bloom, B. S.   134
Bond, T.   157
British Psychological Society (BPS)   2, 23
Carkhuff, R. R.   108
Clements, A. J.   147, 152
CNAA (Council for National Academic
   Awards)   5, 45
Coate, M. A.   110
Deurzen-Smith, E.   35
Dooley, C.   126
Dryden, W.   21, 35, 38, 42, 49, 52, 54, 76,
   108, 129
Egan, G.   35, 87
Ellis, A.   77
Feltham, C.   76
Fonagy, P.   26
Ford, J. D.   90, 93–4
Garfield, S. L.   62, 100
Gibbs, G.   84, 132–3, 136, 139, 141
Glass, G.   62
Godden, D.   122
Goodyear, R. K.   79
Habeshaw, T.   84, 135, 139, 141
Hansen, J. C.   28

Hargie, O.   134
Hepson, B.   134
Higgitt, A.   26
HMI (Her Majesty's Inspectorate)   147
Jacobs, M.   54, 89, 135
Jones, J. E.   105
Kagan, M.   95
Kagan, N.   53, 94, 95
Lambert, M. J.   30
Lebow, J. L.   75
McMahon, G.   127
Mahrer, A. R.   26, 27
Marriage Guidance Council (MGC)   5
Mearns, D.   35, 84, 100, 105, 128, 129
Menzies, I. E. P.   34
Miller, T.   62
Nelson-Jones, R.   26, 70
Noyes, E.   1
OFSTED (Office for Standards in
   Education)   147
Pearce, J. S.   147, 152
Persaud, R.   108
Pfeiffer, J. W.   105
Reber, A. S.   26, 27
Rogers, C. R.   34
Rowntree, D.   41, 47, 132, 133, 134, 139,
   141, 148, 150, 153, 154
Samuels, A.   34
Scally, M.   134
Simosko, S.   143
Smith, M.   62
Sue, D.   79
Sue, D. W.   79
Thorne, B.   35, 42, 52
Trower, P.   35
United Kingdom Council for
   Psychotherapy (UKCP)   2
Verba, S.   48
Wallace, W. A.   31
Windt, P. Y.   126
Woolfe, R.   80
Youngman, M. B.   153

# Subject Index

academic judgements, and appeals procedures 142–3
accommodation 51–2
accountability
  and evaluation 145, 147, 157
  and professional development 127–8
accreditation, of professional counsellor training courses 9
Accreditation of Prior Learning see APL
admission 3, 13, 55–74
  application forms 63–4
  application process 59–69
  and core theoretical model 37–8, 62, 63–4
  course booklets 57–8
  induction into course 73–4
  publicizing course 55–6
  see also selection procedures
advertising counselling courses 56
Advice, Guidance and Counselling Lead Body (AGCLB) 23
age of applicants, and selection procedures 62, 63
APL (Accreditation of Prior Learning) 3, 7, 22, 23, 143
appeals procedures 20, 142–3
application forms 63–4
approach-specific skills 35, 86–7
assessment 3, 14, 131, 132–44
  appeals procedures 20, 142–3
  boards 138
  borderline categories 138, 140
  of client work 108, 114–15, 141, 142
  of competence to practise 136
  controlled and open methods 139
  and core theoretical model 14, 38, 135, 136, 139
  of course content 135–6
  deferred work 141–2
  by external examiners 137–8
  feedback 132, 133–4, 142
  formative 132, 133–4
  methods 138–40
  oral examinations 138
  and personal development groups 103–4
  of practical counselling skills 134–5
  and profiling 141
  recording level achieved 140–1
  referred work 141
  scheme contents 141–2
  self-assessment 104, 137
  summative 132, 133, 134–44
  written examinations 139, 140
attitude scales, embryonic 70
audiotapes 53
  and assessment 135, 139
  in skills training 89, 91, 93, 95
  and supervision 122
audiovisual aids
  in demonstrations 84
  in lectures 82
autobiographies, as pre-course writing task 73
BAC (British Association for Counselling) 2
  Accreditation Sub-Committee 4, 9
  appeals and complaints procedures 154–5, 156
  and assessment 136
  and client work 112–13, 114, 115
  code of ethics 81–2, 157
  and core theoretical model 25–6, 28
  course recognition scheme 3–9, 17, 22
  and course staff 43
  and evaluation 146, 147
  membership 128
  and personal development groups 103
  and personal journals 104
  and phased counselling training 20
  and pre-interview consultations 65
  scholarship fund 58–9

and selection criteria for courses   13,
   59–60
and staff–student contact hours   19
and supervision   117, 118, 119, 123,
   124–5
and training placements   110
Working Party   4–6, 7
*see also* CRG
Behavioural counselling   38
behavioural skills, assessment   135
brainstorming   83–4
bursaries   42
Carnegie Trust   59
CATS (Credit Accumulation Transfer
   Scheme)   22–3
change   15
   and core theoretical model   32–3
   and personality theories   26, 27
client work   3, 107–16
   assessment of   108, 114–15, 141, 142
   and core theoretical model   35–6, 107,
      108, 110, 112, 116
   during counselling courses   113
   counselling placements   109–14
   cultures of clients   129
   100 supervised hours   114
   keeping a log of   115–16
   numbers of clients seen   115
   and professional development   126,
      127, 129–30
   psychopathology in clients   108, 115
   range of clients seen   114
   readiness to see clients   107–9
   self in relation to clients   99
   and self-development   109
   and skills training   87, 107
   social context of clients   78–80
   specific client problems   80–1
   student opportunities for   14
   and supervision   113, 114, 115, 122–3,
      124–5
   *see also* counselling placements
clinical responsibility, and counselling
   placements   111
clinical supervision   3

codes of ethics   15
cognitive skills, assessment   134, 135
Cognitive-Behavioural counselling   34–5,
   38, 86
coherence of training   16
cohorts, integrity of   17–18
community meetings   105, 131, 155
competitive interviews   66–7
complaints mediators   10, 47–8, 147,
   155–6
complaints procedures   10, 154–6
consumer protection, and BAC-recognized
   courses   9–10
contracts, for counselling placements   112
coping model, of skills training   90–1
core theoretical model   3, 13, 14, 24,
   25–40
   and admission   37–8, 62, 63–4
   and alternative models   14–15, 33–4,
      77–8
   and assessment   14, 38, 135, 136, 139
   assumptions about being human   31–2
   and BAC   25–6, 28
   and client work   35–6, 107, 108, 110,
      112, 116
   and CRG   7, 25–6
   and evaluation   14, 38
   function   28–31
   influence on theory   14, 31–5
   'model' or 'theory' of counselling   27
   process of learning   75–7
   professional counsellor training based on
      16, 17
   and professional development   30
   and self-development   30, 36–7, 103,
      106
   and sexual orientation issues   58
   and skills training   14, 35, 85, 86–7, 95
   and social systems   34–5
   and specific client problems   34
   and staff recruitment   44
   and supervision   36, 43–4, 119–20
costs of training   42
   in course booklets   57
   deposit-paying applicants   70–1

obtaining financial help   42, 58–9
paying for selection interviews   66
counselling placements   109–14
    contracts   112
    and counselling opportunities   109–10
    placement agencies   110–12
    supervision by   117–18
counselling psychologists, and research
    23
counselling skills
    assessment   134–5
    and client work   108–9
    nature   85–6
    in other professions   21
    tests   70
    see also skills training
counsellor trainers
    and assessment   133
    and career progression   44
    and core theoretical model   30
    and personal development groups
        103–4
    qualifications and experience   43–4
    self-evaluation   150–1
    and skills training   88–9
    support and development   49–50
    see also staffing
counter-transference   33
course booklets   57–8
course consultants   46–7
course handbook for students   73, 155
course leaders   44–5
course teams   41–2
Courses Recognition Group see CRG
Credit Accumulation Transfer Scheme see
    CATS
CRG  (Courses Recognition Group)
    6–7, 8, 9, 10–11, 12, 22
    and APL   23, 143
    and client work   14, 113
    and core theoretical model   7, 25–6
    on eclective and integrative courses
        39–40
    and external mediators   47
    and research   24

and supervision   36
deaf applicants   58
demonstrations   84
disabled students   68
discrimination training   89–90
eclectic approaches   6
    core theoretical model   28, 38–40, 78
economic viability, and quality assurance
    4
educational developments, and professional
    counsellor training   22–3
effectiveness, and evaluation   148
elements of professional counsellor train-
    ing   3, 6–7, 13–15
    influence of core theoretical model
        31–5
empathy   85, 93, 135
engagement, in counselling process   33
equal opportunities   58
    and interviewing applicants   69
essays
    as assessment methods   139
    submitted by applicants   69, 71
ethics
    breach of   129
    code of   81–2, 130, 157
evaluation   3, 14, 145–57
    annual audits/reviews   147, 148–9, 153
    checklists   152
    complaints   154–6
    and core theoretical model   14, 38
    and effectiveness   148
    and feedback   146, 148, 154–5
    formal   152–3
    formative   151
    informal   151–2
    observation   152–3
    questionnaires   153
    of specific parts of course   149–50
    structured reviews   152
    summative   151
    use of information   153–4
Existential counselling   34, 35, 38
external examiners   46
    assessment by   137–8

evaluation by 147
feedback
  and assessment 132, 133–4, 142
  and evaluation 146, 148, 154–5
  in skills training 88, 90, 93–5
  and unsuccessful applicants 72–3
fees, course recognition 9
financial help, obtaining 58–9
formative assessment 132, 133–4
formative evaluation 151
full-time courses, and CRG 7
Gestalt therapy, approach-specific skills 86
grants 58–9
group discussion tasks 69–70
groups
  buzz groups 83
  discussion groups 84
  group supervision 87–8, 120–1, 123
  personal development groups 97, 101–4, 128, 131, 133
handouts for students 83
health care, counselling growth within 2
health workers, and counselling skills training 21
imitation, in skills training 91
in-house counselling training courses 21
indemnity insurance 128
individual differences, and self-development 100
individualized interviews 66–7
individuals, and social context 79
institutional settings 80
integrative approaches 6, 26
  core theoretical model 28, 38–40, 78
interviews, selecting course applicants 65–9
IPR (Interpersonal Process Recall) 94–5
journals
  advertising counselling courses in 56
  personal 97, 104, 133
  professional 5, 127, 131
language tests, for overseas students 71
learning
  approaches to 82–4

and assessment 136, 139
  self as a learner 99
lectures 82–3
length of courses, and CRG 7
library provision 52–3
line management supervision 118–19
Masters courses in counselling 20–1, 69
mastery model, of skills training 90–1
mental health care
  counselling growth within 2
  and professional development 128
  working with other professionals in 82
'model' of counselling 27
National Vocational Qualifications see NVQs
newspapers, advertising counselling courses in 56
NVQs (National Vocational Qualifications) 23
observation, evaluation by 152–3
organizational settings 80, 127
overseas students, language tests for 71
part-time counselling courses 67
  and client work 113, 114
pattern change 33, 87
pattern search 33, 86–7
peer assessment 104
peer counselling 91–2
peer supervision, of counsellor trainers 150–1
Person-Centred counselling
  assessment methods 139
  and core theoretical model 30, 34, 35, 38
  and personal development 103
  and professional development 37
  and skills training 86, 95
personal development see self-development
personal development groups 97, 101–4, 128, 131, 133
personal growth
  and applicants for courses 60, 61, 62, 68
  and self-development 105
personal journals 97, 104, 133

'personal record', of students 14
personal therapy
 and course applicants 60
 for students 97, 100–1
 and assessment 136, 141
 and core theoretical model 36–7
 and skills training 92
personality, of applicants for courses
 62–3, 67, 72–3
personality tests, of applicants 70
personality theories, and counselling 26–7
phased counselling training 19, 20–1
political questions, analysis of 80
portfolios, and APL 143
practice, codes of 157
primary health care, counselling growth
 within 2
private practices, and professional development 126–7
private training organizations, and evaluation 147
professional bodies
 codes of ethics 157
 and evaluation 146–7
 membership 128
 see also BAC
professional development 3, 15, 125,
 126–31
 assessment 135
 codes of ethics 15
 and core theoretical model 30, 37
 curriculum 130
 evaluating 148
 and supervision 126, 131
'professional log', of client work 14
professional practice 81–2
profiling 141
Psychodynamic theory 34
 and group supervision 120–1
 and personal development 37
psychological disturbance/well-being, and
 core theoretical models 32
psychopathology in clients 108, 115
psychotherapists, courses staffed by 43
publicizing courses 55–6

quality assurance
 and economic viability 4
 and evaluation 145, 147
 and professional development 127
questionnaires, evaluation by 153
Rational Emotive Behaviour Therapy
 (REBT) 29, 33, 35, 108
 approach-specific skills 86
 and professional development 37
 self-development activities 37
reality, social construction of 79, 129,
 130, 131
recognition of professional counsellor
 training courses 5, 9
references 64–5
reflective practitioners, development as
 157
re-recognition, courses applying for 8–9
research 23–4
resources 3, 51–4
response training 89–90
role-plays 14
scholarships 58–9
Scottish Vocational Qualifications see
 SVQs
selection procedures 13, 59–63
 and age of applicants 62, 63
 and applicant's development as a counsellor 61
 BAC guidelines 13, 59–60
 and client work 109
 conditions on offer of places 71
 deposit-paying applicants 70–1
 feedback to unsuccessful applicants
 72–3
 group discussion tasks 69–70
 induction into course 73–4
 interviews 65–9
 personality of applicants 62–3
 and personality tests 70
 pre-interview consultations 65
 and prior academic achievement 61
 and prior counselling experience/train-
 ing 60–1
 'process review' 69–70

references 64–5
submission of essays 69, 71
uncertainty regarding 71–2
self-assessment 104, 137
self-awareness work 14
self-development 3, 16, 97–106
  aims 98–100
  assessment of 136
  BAC guidelines on 13–14
  and client work 109
  and community meetings 105
  and core theoretical model 30, 36–7,
    103, 106
  and extension of life experience 105
  and individual differences 100
  personal development groups 97,
    101–4, 128, 131, 133
  personal journals 97, 104
  and professional development 126
  and skills training 21
  spirit of 106
self-evaluation 150–1
sexual orientation issues 58
'skilled helper' model 87
skills training 3, 14, 84, 85–96
  approach-specific skills 35, 86–7
  and assessment 133, 134–5
  and core theoretical model 14, 35, 85,
    86–7, 95
  discrimination and response training
    89–90
  feedback 88, 90, 93–5
  informal 87–8
  instruction 90
  integration of skills 95–6
  IPR (Interpersonal Process Recall) 94–5
  modelling 90–1
  practice 90, 91–3
    and self-development 98
  and professional development 126
  role-playing in 92–3
  staff–student ratios 18, 88
  and supervision 87–8, 95
  timing 87–8
  video recordings 53–4

*see also* counselling skills
'snowballing' technique 83
social construction of reality 79, 129, 130,
  131
social control 80
social differences 79–80
social systems
  and core theoretical models 34–5
  influence on behaviour 15
social workers
  and counselling skills training 21
  seeking careers in counselling 59
special needs, of course applicants 68
specialized counselling training courses
  21–2
staff–student contact hours, BAC guidelines 19
staff–student ratios 18–19, 42
  BAC guidelines 18–19
  for skills training 18, 88
staff–student relationships
  and assessment 104
  and core theoretical model 30
staffing 3, 41–54
  and assessment 133, 136–8
  and codes of ethics 157
  complaints mediators 10, 47–8, 147,
    155–6
  course consultants 46–7
  course leaders 44–5
  course teams 41–3, 154
  and evaluation 145–6, 147, 148–9,
    153–4
  ex-students as staff 44
  external examiners 46, 137–8, 147
  and pastoral work 45
  qualifications and experience 42–4
  roles and responsibilities 44–6
  staff meetings 48
  staff offices 52
  staff support and development 49–50
  *see also* counsellor trainers
stress
  and counsellor trainers 49
  and trainees 128–9

students
    assessment 3, 14, 131, 132–44
    client work 3, 107–16
    course handbook for 73–4
    disruption to personal and social life 68
    drop-outs 17, 55
    and evaluation 146, 147, 148, 154
    handouts for 83
    increasing student numbers 51
    induction into the course 73–4
    integrity of student cohorts 17–18
    peer counselling 91–2
    and personal therapy 36–7, 92, 97,
      100–1, 136, 141
    and pre-interview consultations 65
    self-development 3, 16, 97–106
    and sexual orientation issues 58
    with special needs 68
    supervision 14, 117–25
    *see also* staff–student ratios; staff-student
      relationships
sufficiency guidelines, and supervision
    123–5
summative assessment 132, 133, 134–44
summative evaluation 151
supervision 14, 117–25
    approaches to 121–3
    and assessment 133, 135
    and BAC code of ethics 81–2
    and career progression 44
    and client work 113, 114, 115, 122–3,
      124–5
    and core theoretical model 36, 43–4,
      119–20
    counselling agency supervision 117–18
    and counselling placements 111
    and CRG 7
    and evaluation 149
    group supervision 120–1, 124
    individual personal supervision
      118–20, 124
    line management supervision 118–19
    lists of 'approved' supervisors 119

    and personal development 97, 103
    and professional development 126, 131
    and skills training 87–8, 95
    staff–student ratios 18
    and stress 128
    sufficiency guidelines 123–5
    theory of 82
    and trainer self-evaluation 150–1
SVQs (Scottish Vocational Qualifications)
    23
teachers, and counselling skills training 21
teaching, approaches to 82–4
termination, in counselling process 33
theory 3, 14–15, 16, 75–84
    alternative models 14–15, 33–4, 77–8
    approaches to teaching and learning
      82–4
    clinical practice issues 82
    and professional development 126
    social context 78–80
    and social systems 15
    staff–student ratios 18
    *see also* core theoretical model
trainee trainers, and skills training 89
trainees *see* students
trainers *see* counsellor trainers; staffing
transference 33, 85, 127
universities
    and appeals procedures 142
    counselling courses in 52
    counselling courses seeking validation
      by 53
    and evaluation 146, 147
    and prior academic achievement of
      applicants 61
    professional counsellor training in 3–4
video recordings 53–4
    and assessment 135, 139
    of interviews with role-playing 'clients'
      70
    in skills training 89, 91, 93, 95
    and supervision 121, 122
word-of-mouth publicity 55–6

HALESOWEN COLLEGE
LIBRARY